# RE-SCRIPTING your LiFe!

## *Power Principles for True Happiness*

## Dr. Suzette Clements

Decatur, GA

Address inquiries to the publisher:

Highest You Publishing
4920 Flat Shoals Pkwy
Suite 102 Box 229
Decatur, Georgia 30034 USA

Learn more about the author at
www.HighestYou.com

ISBN: 978-0-9908257-2-2

Library of Congress Control Number: 2014917021

Printed in the United States of America

Edited by Annette R. Johnson, Allwrite Communications

# DEDICATION

*This book is dedicated to my mom who, despite her rough beginnings of losing her mom at age 2 and never knowing her father, became one of the most beautiful, powerful and influential people in her community and in the lives of generations. To my dad, who influenced us with principles of wisdom and success, and a love for making people feel significant. They proved to me over and over that all things are possible if only you believe in yourself and the power of God to work in and through you.*

# PREFACE

Do you want more passion in your life?

Do you want to know you make a difference?

Do you want to know your life matters?

Do you want more happiness in your life?

I have been on a personal quest to answer these questions in the affirmative. I have stumbled on such wonderful information and feel I must share it with you since it has transformed my very existence.

This book is in your possession right now because you too may have been asking similar questions. The wondrous thing about this amazing journey called life is that when we are ready to walk into our destiny, everything in the universe begins lining up with us. Miraculously, things that once seemed difficult and unattainable, all of a sudden become easy and effortless. One word or action in the direction of your dream and your life takes a drastic shift in the right direction. Is this luck? Could it be faith or the favor of God? Perhaps, it's karma. There are many belief systems around this topic.

The purpose of this book is to challenge you, the reader, to see your role in your life. Does life deal you blows that keep knocking you down? Are you stuck in unhappy relationships that no longer serve you? Do you quietly believe that there must be more to life than what you are currently seeing or experiencing? What you must realize and I emphasize is that you can change any situation as long as you believe you can and understand how to effectively employ the principles in this book.

My agenda is quite simple. It's to share principles that I and countless others have incorporated into our lives to shape our world for the better.

I recommend that you read this book several times. Underline key points. Highlight! Write on the margins. Do whatever it takes to make this information memorable and applicable. At the end of each chapter, there are exercises to help you incorporate the principles covered. Do these exercises to get and reinforce the desired results. They will only work if they work through you. Knowledge of a thing is wonderful, but application of that knowledge is needed to re-script your life.

# CONTENTS

# ACKNOWLEDGMENTS

I am grateful to my husband, Kirby Jr., for loving me deeply and sincerely. Your wisdom and integrity are rare, and you embody and share them with such eloquence. To our son, Kirby III, thanks for staying true to you and choosing your own path. It has been a pure delight seeing you mature into manhood. You have a gentle and open heart that is rare and beautiful. To our daughter, Gabrielle, I appreciate your pure love, authenticity and honesty. You are a constant reminder of God's unconditional love.

# 1

# BEGIN AT THE END

We, as human beings, are amazing works of art who have unlimited potential and possibilities. The most beautiful part is that WE play the key role. Yes, the "key role." We are magnificent human and spiritual beings who have the ability to guide our lives by the choices we make every minute of every day. We do this either proactively or reactively. What do I mean by that?

Good and bad things happen to us every day. Just listen to the news and you quickly become flooded with information of tragedy, fighting, loss, and despair. Every now and then, a story of triumph is thrown our way that brings hope. What is my point? Stuff happens! It happens to us all. Tragedy does not discriminate. It (stuff) is like rain. It simply falls. If you happen to be in its path, it falls on you. Thus, the phrase it rains "on the just and the unjust" (Matt. 5:45) shows that the event does not define the individual. It is not the tragedy or event that determines our destiny, but it is our response to the event. Yes, our ability to respond to the situations in our lives determines the life we live. We all know or at least have heard of people who, despite insurmountable struggles and apparent defeat, pushed onward and have lived victoriously.

I once heard a story of two bed-ridden men who were hospitalized and sharing a room. One patient occupied the bed next to a window and looked out every day giving the other patient, who occupied the bed closest to the door, a report. Every day, the patient closest to the window would tell of lovely images that he saw. They became very close friends until one day the patient close to the window had difficulties and died. Although he was very sad, the patient who had occupied the bed by the door asked if he could be moved to the window bed so he too could see the wonderful things that his roommate had shared with him. To his surprise, the view was that of a cold brick building that had absolutely none of the beautiful things that he'd been described. This patient could not understand why his former roommate would lie to him. When he inquired of the nurse, he was told that the gentleman who had become his best friend and constant source of encouragement, had been a blind patient. All of the wonderful things he, the blind patient, shared with the patient closest to the door were based on his imagination.

I share this story to say that we never know what other people are going through. It is important to gather as much information as possible when permitted. We can and therefore must choose to live our lives with great vision and hope despite its current manifestations. It is very easy to judge our lives from the perspective of another. We may see a married couple and wish to be like them only to find out later that they had significant difficulty. It's easy to look at other people and want what they have, not realizing the sacrifice that came before their success. I call this "the grass is always greener on the other side syndrome." The takeaway here is that perception is in the eye of the beholder. What we perceive to be true becomes our truth. In chapter 8, I will go into much detail on sharpening your perception.

Let me share how my perception became my truth. It has been my belief that we should teach the thing we need to learn the most. I passionately teach the art of happiness because I felt empty, insecure and lonely. How could this be me? From the outside looking in, my life could be perceived as perfect. I was a doctor, married to a lawyer who also happened to be my college sweetheart. He was my first boyfriend, and I was his first girlfriend. We dated for seven years before marriage and had two wonderful, healthy children. We are both entrepreneurs who operate our own practices. So, why would anyone in my shoes even dare to entertain depressing feelings? After all, we were the inverse of the Huxtables. I was Cliff, and Kirby was Clair. However, The Clements Show was not looking anything like *The Cosby Show*. Why, you ask? Let me share why.

At age 38, while at the crest of my career, I developed full-blown menopause. It's a very difficult thing to explain what a woman's body goes through during this "change of life." Every single aspect of my body felt as if it was falling apart. My mind was slow, my memory was foggy, and my emotions were more erratic than a rollercoaster at Six Flags.

I also developed the worse case of depression that I've ever experienced. I consider myself normally happygo-lucky, cheerful, positive, and uplifting, but when these changes took place, that person went on a very long vacation. I could see myself going through the changes, but I felt somewhat limited to gain control. I felt as if I was submerged under water with the ability to see the top but no means of getting there. This proved to be very frustrating. You see, throughout my entire life up until this point, I had been able to set my mind to whatever I wanted and go in that direction to attain it.

After graduating from high school, I set my sights for Oral Roberts University. This was great except for the fact that I had no financial means of attending. I remember writing my vision and intending that this was what I wanted to do. **I began with the end in mind**. Once the vision was written, I called the school and spoke to one of the financial aid counselors. To my surprise, she said the following words, "Go ahead and come and we'll see what we can do." That's all I needed to hear. In less than one week, I was on a Greyhound bus with $150 and a suitcase to Tulsa, Oklahoma. My brother-in-law Roy brought me to the bus station and wished me well. That was perhaps the longest Greyhound ride I've ever taken. Actually, it was the only Greyhound ride I've taken. Fast forward… I graduated with my bachelor of science in nursing and met the love of my life.

I was a go-getter and saw little to no obstacles in my late teens and early 20s. I would write my vision and move in the direction of the vision and miraculously all things would line up. Oral Roberts would teach over and over to expect a miracle, and that's how I lived my life. Thus, you can imagine how I felt when the heavy cloud of depression landed on me. I didn't know who this person was occupying my body. The avatar was the same, but someone else was driving.

I now teach the Art of Happiness because I had to find my joy again. I teach what I spent years looking for. I have often said, "If I were my husband, I would have left me during my menopausal turmoil." That's how bad things were. Nevertheless, he was a trooper, and he stuck by me through thick and thin, showing me true unconditional love. I believe that's the "better or worse" part of the marriage vows we exchanged on our wedding day. I'm sure many people say those vows but never expect them to be challenged. I'm so glad that when we said them, we meant them, and at this most difficult time in my life, he was able to commit to his word and love me despite my tumultuous menopausal changes.

## Co-Creating

I believe we are here on earth to live life to the fullest. We are here to procreate and co-create. Co-creation is the act of producing something that already existed in another form; it's a molding, rather than making, process. I use "co-creating" versus "creating" because it is my belief that creation itself is complete. We have everything needed to achieve whatever we are purposed to do. We simply need to access and utilize the resources, which can still be in the unseen, or invisible, realm. An airplane is not created. It is co-created by taking thoughts and ideas out of the invisible realm and manifesting it in our physical realm. In essence, we take thought substance and transform it to physical substance. We are taking "what is" and converting it into a new thing. Utilizing a principle of thermodynamics that says energy can neither be created nor destroyed; we simply, through the process of co-creation, make an energy exchange.

We collaborate with our infinite source defined as God, The Universe, Infinite Spirit, Our Father, Mother-Father God, The Great I AM, to name a few, and take what "IS" out of the unseen realm to manifest it into the seen realm. Jesus manifested along his path everything he needed. We too have this ability. Napoleon Hill in his book, Think And Grow Rich, said, *"I ask not for divine providence or more riches, but more wisdom with which to accept and use wisely the riches I received at birth in the form of the power to control and direct my mind to whatever ends I desire."*

Once I became aware that I had a significant part in co-creating my life, many light bulbs came on, providing answers as well as questions. What was I doing well but could do more of? What beliefs was I holding that were limiting my forward momentum? Who were my teammates in this game of life? Could I change the sport I was playing? Was I playing baseball with football rules? Did my teammates share my commitment and values? The questions just flooded my mind. I had to take a good evaluation of my current status in life and see what choices, good or bad, I had made to bring me where I was. All my questions had one similar answer. It was not only the circumstances that I encountered, but more importantly, it was my response to life's circumstances that guided and directed my life.

As a Doctor of Podiatric Medicine, DPM, I know that before medications are released as prescriptions, they must go through a lengthy, rigorous process of testing. Before they are used for the general population, typically small or large trials are done. These studies are done to compare the effects of a medication on the individual compared to an individual not taking the medication. These double blind studies have such incredible results that, at times, the study is stopped so all participants can benefit and not only the ones taking the medication. Another positive outcome is that sometimes the participants who got the placebo (having no medicinal value at all) will also begin having the desired results simply because they BELIEVE they are getting the medication. They begin having similar positive reactions as if they were actually taking the medication.

I put myself on a trial test medication. Being armed with the knowledge that I could co-create my life, I set out to do just that. I had much emotional turmoil and felt extremely unhappy during menopause. At times, I felt despondent and even depressed. I began praying and asking God to help me.

*"I ask not for divine providence or more riches, but more wisdom with which to accept and use wisely the riches I received at birth in the form of the power to control and direct my mind to whatever ends I desire."*

*-Napoleon Hill*

This book chronicles my journey out of misery to a place of peace and happiness. Once I began taking the test medication (re-scripting my life), I began feeling better so fast that I wanted to stop the research and allow others to benefit from the medication as soon as possible.

I have found that certain principles are true across the board, and when applied to our lives, tangible changes take place. Some of these changes are negative and some are positive based on the beliefs we hold at the time of the event. I'll explain more about this later.

Let me give a disclaimer. Am I saying that my life has mainly been a bed of roses? Absolutely not. Actually, quite the contrary. I sometimes feel like I've been fighting an uphill battle and just found out I have wings. These wings can take me to my desired destination somewhat easily and effortlessly. It's almost as if I were Dorothy in the *Wizard of Oz* and just realized all the things I went looking for were always in my possession. It looks as if I truly have everything I need. This acknowledgement is significant since, throughout my life, I have been taught that "The Lord is my shepherd, and I have everything I need." I heard this over and over at church and while growing up. I spoke it, but for the first time, I realized its true personal significance.

What am I saying? This sums it up, not hidden in language you can't understand. Be alert right now. If you understand and apply what I am going to impart, it can and will transform your life. You don't even have to believe me or what is said for it to work. You only need to apply the principles. Every part of this book may not be for you at this stage of your journey, so use the parts that relate and leave the rest. The fact that you are in possession of this book means that you are doing something right. Whether you realize it or not, you had a part of bringing this book into your life. More on that later. Let's get back to the point I am making.

I am saying that our lives are for us to live to the fullest by co-creating. Yes, we have input in the direction of our lives. We have this ability through the power of our choices. Because we make a tremendous amount of choices daily in the form of habits, we often overlook our input. It's like we have gone on auto pilot and forgot that we are also the co-pilot of our lives. I once heard someone say that we plan more for vacations than we do for our lives. This is often true for most people until they learn and apply the principles in this book.

## Knowing the Destination

This chapter focuses on the simple fact that if we have a say in the direction of our lives, we must then be astute about the journey to the destination or endpoint. Any pilot knows that he or she must first have the destination before beginning a journey. Care is taken to determine the route, the distance, the cost, and even how many passengers to take.

Living in Georgia gives us constant access to Hartsfield-Jackson International Airport, the busiest airport in the world. On any given day, this process is seen over and over. Planes take off and land, all going in various directions. Multiple runways are used. Tremendous planning is necessary to avoid overlap or accidents. Many systems are in place to keep a constant flow of the airplanes and prevent bottlenecks.

Pilots must know their destination before taking off. Otherwise, they will either never take off or they will wander aimlessly, eventually running out of resources, such as fuel. Knowing where you are going allows you to make the proper preparation, including the best route. How long is the trip? How much fuel is needed? How many passengers can be carried?

My brother-in-law Fred is a pilot and says that beginning with the destination in mind is a must and a crucial aspect of all aviation or the travel industry in general. When applying this principle to our lives, the same is true. How do we begin the process of re-scripting our lives? Well, we must determine where we want to go, or where we want to end. In other words, what would my new and improved life look like? Could I be healthier, wealthier and travel more with my family and friends? Could I be happier and more self-actualized? Could I have better and more supportive relationships in my life? Could I drive that cherry red BMW? Could my children be people of excellence in their chosen fields? The possibilities are endless and the answer to all of these questions is an astounding YES!

## Simple Beginnings

Before I go any further, let me share a little about me and my journey. I believe it's important to understand where I am coming from to get the most out of this book. First of all, I am an alien. Yes, you heard me right, an alien, not from another planet, but from another country. I was born on the little but beautiful island of Jamaica. I am the youngest of seven children. We were all delivered at home by nurse midwives. Needless to say, I have much respect for my mom for pushing through to the end. No pun intended.

My parents were simple, yet profound, pillars of the community where we grew up, and they helped shape the foundation and belief system as well as the success of several cities. My parents lived what they believed and believed what they lived. From them, I learned the value of persistence, being a person of excellence, and caring for those less fortunate. My dad would often say, "Sue, no matter what your hands find to do, always do it to the best of your ability as unto God, whether you're being watched or not." He would often say, "Even if

*"Knowledge of a thing is wonderful, but application of that knowledge is needed."*

*-Suzette Clements*

you're sweeping the floor, do it with excellence." Although my parents, by today's standards, were not financially wealthy, they were world changers with the little that they had. They helped the less fortunate. Both my parents were entrepreneurs and mentored others in their trades. My mom was a seamstress, and my dad was a painter. They both passed on their wisdom and expertise to groups and individuals, helping them establish their own businesses.

I tell you all of this because even though we began with what many would consider little, we were rich in principle and integrity. From this humble and honest upbringing, I came to understand that I could do or be anything. My motto in my 20s was "if they can do it, I can do it also." I remember sitting at New York College of Podiatric Medicine in the fall of 1996 and saying those exact words to encourage myself. It was the first day of podiatric medical school, and I realized that I was amongst the oldest of the students. In fact, the majority of the other students were significantly younger. Immediately, I began to second-guess myself wondering if I'd made the right choice. What was I thinking? Another four years of school? Then residency? After my heart rate returned to normal and the blood returned to my head, I confidently looked to my left, then looked to my right, and made the statement again. "If they can do it, I can do it also." This became my motto. No matter what difficulty was ahead of me, I would always say this. When it came time for me to do my first surgical procedure, I had to remind myself again. "Others before me had done this successfully, so therefore, I too can do it successfully." And I did.

Being older was actually very advantageous to me. Since I had worked as a nurse, I had a solid clinical background. A lot of things that were new to the other students were second-nature for me since I had had significant exposure to patients already. Not to toot my own horn, but what seemed to be a potential problem for me, as I sat thinking on my first day, turned out to be a huge benefit. We, the older students in the class, were often the highest academic performers. I believe this is because we tended to be more mature and had been in the work field and knew the cost of being diligent versus goofing off. That being said, I graduated in the top third of the class while being a new mother and giving birth to my second child. Again, I mention this not to brag, but to show that with perseverance and commitment what appears to be shortcomings can be used as stepping stones. I, therefore, learned early to use my weaknesses to propel me forward.

During my fourth year in the final week of classes, I went into labor with Gabrielle. This was right before I took my final exam for surgery. My husband, Kirby Jr., called the school to notify them that I was in labor. The person who answered the phone said, "Does this mean she won't be coming to the final?" She was actually serious. He laughed and said, "If things change, I'll let you know." Like my mom, I pushed through to the end and graduated on time with my class and my beautiful baby daughter. Quitting was never in my scripting. It was never even a thought.

Let me backtrack a bit. I had been working in Atlanta as a registered nurse since 1989 at age 23 and found nursing to be very rewarding and fulfilling, but I wanted to diagnose and treat as opposed to fulfilling doctors' orders. I loved being a nurse, but I kept feeling a tug to keep moving. This is when I decided that I wanted to be a doctor and treat patients in my own practice. I did what I'm telling you to do. I wrote my vision of what I wanted. I BEGAN WITH THE END

DESTINATION. My end destination was practicing as a physician in my own practice. Today, I am doing just that.

> *We must CHOOSE to begin*
> *where we want to end.*

## Your Beginnings

You may be asking, "How do I begin moving toward where I want to end if I don't know where I want to end?" This is not a problem. Begin with ONE STEP. That's right, just one step. As a podiatrist, I teach patients who are having various foot related conditions to walk again. I am telling you what I tell them. Take one step and trust that the floor will support you. This is often a most difficult process for patients I treat for ankle fractures and sprains since the ankle has position receptors, which are often disrupted at the time of the injury, that communicate between the body and the ground. The injury coupled with the fact that I have had them in a cast for approximately 6 to 8 weeks lends to temporary distrust that the ankle will support them again. Like I tell them, "I'm telling you now; just take one step." I also tell them their destination, or expected level of recovery, at the beginning of treatment so we both understand the desired outcome. Again, we begin with the end in mind. To date, I have never had a patient who was unable to master the art of learning to walk again. Quite the contrary, they often go on to running and resuming their full physical activities without limitations.

The take home here is that once we define the desired endpoint, we create a care plan or road map to get there. The endpoint is also known as "the vision" or desired "dream." Your vision may involve being in a certain profession, being a certain weight, or perhaps being happily married. SINCE ALL THINGS ARE POSSIBLE, then there must be a process of transforming one's vision into reality; the unseen into the seen; or thoughts into matter.

## Writing the Vision

Write the vision of what you want, your desired outcome or endpoint. Don't worry about how or by what means it will happen. Just begin to write. Take the first step. Dreaming and visualizing is crucial, but we do not stop there. We make a conscious effort and choose to write the vision. The written vision is like a stamp of approval. It gets the ball rolling. The practice of writing is often overlooked. Many people have lofty dreams and visions that never come to fruition because this part of the process is overlooked.

The specific nature of the written vision is important, for the more precise the written vision, the quicker the manifestation from the unseen to the seen. When writing the vision, write it so that anyone who reads your vision, would be able to read it and say, "Oh, that's what you want?"

Others should be able to read the vision without further instructions or explanation. That's how precise it should be. It's kind of how specific a pregnant woman is when she wants a specific food that she is craving. She sends her husband on a baby-craving run and is often very specific by saying, "What the baby must have…" I remember asking my husband to make sure he got exactly the brand and quantity of precisely what I requested. My baby hormones were very specific and I had to convey to my husband with great detail and accuracy so both the baby and I would be happy. I thank God he was patient and supportive. He always got exactly what I craved since he knew failure to do so would mean a return visit or visits to the store. We still laugh about these experiences today.

When you begin this journey of re-scripting your life, don't feel as if you are locked into that which you've written or began on the path of executing. This is the beauty of being human. We have choices and the freedom to choose. Yes, it would be ideal if you could know exactly what you wanted and proceed in a straight line until you achieved it, but often in life, I find that most people have difficulty knowing what they want. Therefore, I recommend at least taking steps in the direction of your desired outcome. Begin moving. That's why it's important to write where you want to end. Once you have your destination, you can now create the roadmap and a timeline of how long it will take to get there. Remember, you are the co-pilot, so you must be conscious in making these life-altering decisions.

At this point, you may be asking, "If I am only the co-pilot, then who is the pilot?" The pilot is that divine source we define as God. Some may differentiate between God, the infinite source, and the universe, but it is my belief that if "God IS," then He/She IS. If God is the whole, then all of creation is simply a part of the whole. Since God is the great I AM, then we, being made is this same image, must begin seeing our own "I AM-ness." In chapter 12, we will further discuss the importance of speaking in the I AM manner on a daily basis.

When I decided in 1994 that I wanted to be a doctor, I didn't know the specific type or even how long it would take. I had the destination but neither the roadmap nor timeline. I began asking questions and doing research. The more questions I asked, the more detailed answers I received. I then learned that it would take me two years to complete my prerequisite premed courses prior to being admitted to any medical school. All the while I kept focused on my desired outcome of being a doctor. I completed the remainder of my premed courses and took the MCAT, the medical school entrance exam. I began interviewing other doctors and my two questions were: Do you like what you do? Would you do it again? The majority of the allopathic doctors (MD and DO) said they would not pursue the same career if they had to do it again since they felt as if they missed out on too much of their family life. This was the number one reason why they would not do it again. However, the podiatrists loved the autonomy and the fact that they could practice in such a broad spectrum concerning the foot and ankle. They could do surgery, dermatology, sports medicine, pediatrics or even senior care focusing on the foot. The quality of family life that I was looking for seemed to best lineup with podiatry. This decision was significant for me since we had not yet started having our children and wanted to be very involved in their lives.

So, to reinforce the point, once I wrote down my desired outcome (vision) and began moving in the direction of where I wanted to end up, things began to unfold and doors began to open. Often, we declare the good that we want but go about planning for the bad situations that might happen. This sounds silly as we read this, but we often do this – self-sabotage. Whatever you prepare for will happen, since this is the law. Law, you say. Why, yes! Everything in this universe is governed by laws. If you are ignorant of the laws for any particular aspect of your life, you will continually miss the mark. This feels like you are going in circles or like you are running on a hamster's wheel. The faster you run, the faster you go, but you never move forward. Can you identify with this image? If so, go ahead and smile. Once you identify patterns like these, which are self-limiting, your success is closer than you think.

## Speaking Life

Writing the vision seems easy at first until you sit down to write it. When I did this initially, I only wrote my vision for my career. In my mid 40s when I reevaluated my vision, I felt the need to include my physical health and well being, mental health, financial abundance, as well as excellence in my relationship with God, myself, my family, my community and the world. I'll be honest; I became very overwhelmed at this point. In chapter 4, I will discuss in detail the power of making great choices, but for now, it's important for me to interject the point here that we are creatures of our choices. Our choices guide our experiences and our lives. Because I believe there is a law of choice, I am careful when I sit to re-script my life. Not only are our thoughts and choices significant, but our words are also equally powerful.

As a surgeon, my word is extremely powerful. When I'm in the operating room, my eyes stay focused on the operative field, which is the foot. I speak to my operative team, which typically consists of an anesthesiologist at the head of the bed, a nurse passing me the instruments, and a circulating nurse who maintains the room's ambience and acquires the things I need that may not be in the room. What do I mean by my words are powerful? Well, I speak and immediately the things I ask for are placed in my right hand. I remain focused on the operative field at all times, making sure to perform careful dissection of the tissue while avoiding and maintaining the integrity of the blood vessels and the nerves. I speak the word "retract" and exactly that happens. I say, "Table up," and guess what? The operative table begins to rise and someone says, "Say when," meaning say when it's high enough to stop going up. This operation room dance can be beautiful, fluid and effortless or it can be chaotic with curse words and instruments flying.

I remember while doing my vascular surgery rotation during my second year residency assignment. I was assigned with an attending physician who was brilliant. Within 10 minutes of beginning the case, it was as if all hell broke loose. He called for "mosquito," which is a small instrument used to clamp. This instrument was not available on the tray, however. After what seemed to be a lifetime of waiting, it was finally delivered to his right hand. After fumbling with it, he looked up from his glasses, took both hands to break the defective instrument, and threw it to the floor. He again reached out his right hand and said "mosquito" while refocusing on the operative field. You see, as a surgeon, every second is valuable. Anything that slows your operative progress could potentially harm your patient. Your spoken word is a verbal order that must command an immediate response as well.

The operative room, also known as the OR, is no place for indecisiveness. The most successful surgeons have their trained team with them to anticipate their desires and needs. When this is in place, even the most difficult procedures appear effortless in your life. You may not be a surgeon, but the roles you play such as parent, spouse, boss, colleague, coworker, team member or student are equally important. Granted you don't have to worry that the patient is approaching the maximum anesthesia time while the surgical procedure is needing more time, but the direction you give your team is crucial to the success of everyone. Imagine a teacher without a lesson plan. Can we say pandemonium? Imagine if he or she had an emergency and the substitute teacher had to take over. This would be difficult without a lesson plan in place. Imagine the lack of continuity in the curriculum.

So what's the take-home? The beginning point to re-scripting your life is knowing what you want then staying focused on that vision. As easy as this may sound, most people don't know what they want out of life. Some know what they want but soon lose focus. I became a successful surgeon by staying focused on the operative field while in the operating room. I have also built a core team who has worked well with me and I with them. This relationship between me and the team grew from excellent communication, proper expectations, appropriate follow through, and the dedication of all parties involved. These traits are common in any relationship that is progressing toward excellence. Establishing and purposefully constructing a core support team is crucial to success. But even more crucial is first the realization of the end destination or vision.

## Living by the Laws

Over the past 30 years in the healthcare field, I would ask patients if they could have anything they wanted, what would it be? I was always amazed how many people genuinely didn't know what they wanted. They somehow felt life was something that happened to them and not through them. They didn't see themselves as having an active role in the co-creation of their lives. They were more or less reactionary to life circumstances and therefore basically drifted from circumstance to circumstance.

I believe there's an unspoken law of purpose, which I'll discuss in chapter 2 in detail. It is my belief that this law governs how we live our lives. As we re-script or rewrite our lives, it is crucial that we understand this law and how it works, or at least how it affects us. The laws around the principle of electricity are the same in all parts of the world and operate the same for whomever uses them. Although you may not know the ins and outs of Ohm's law, which relates $V=IR$, or voltage $(V)$ is equal to current $(I)$ multiplied by resistance $(R)$, you do understand the consequences when electricity is properly used or misused. My point here is although we don't know the science behind the law of electricity, we use it on a daily basis to govern our affairs. The next chapter will go into more detail on the significance of laws and how they impact our lives.

# Chapter 1 Written Assignment

*(This is best done early in the morning or late at night. Pick a time when you can be uninterrupted for at least 20 minutes.)*

1. Sit quietly, take several deep breaths and clear your mind.
2. List the top seven areas is in your life you want to re-write (Example: health, relationships, personal growth, wealth, happiness, family, relationship with self, others, community, world, God.) Remember, be true to you. Write what you want, not what you believe someone else wants for you. Be honest with yourself. **Caution:** Other people's voice will try to talk to you here, but stay committed to your dream. Nothing is too silly. Write as if God is sitting next to you smiling and saying, "My dear, what is your heart's desire?"

1. _____
2. _____
3. _____
4. _____
5. _____
6. _____
7. _____

Rewrite the above list in the order of highest priority to least priority. You can add as many as you need or do as few as you like. The point is to realize that you can make significant change in your life.

1. _____

2. _____

3. _____

4. _____

5. _____

6. _____

7. _____

# 2

# THE POWER OF OUR LAWS

Understanding that the universe is governed by laws will help you make the process of re-scripting your life more realistic and attainable. Nature is a wonderful teacher, and I find that when I have difficulty seeing something that is still in the vision phase, I use nature or seen things to help me.

There are so many laws that are working in our lives right now that we just take them for granted. For instance, as you read or listen to this book, chances are you are sitting on a bed or chair all due to the law of gravity. You may not understand Newton's universal law of gravitation, but you appreciate its impact if you hold a pen in your hand and release it. It will fall to the ground or on the surface of first resistance. The law of love, meanwhile, affects how we relate to ourselves and others. The law of physics says that if you sit, you won't move, meaning that a body at rest stays at rest and a body in motion stays in motion. The economic laws of supply and demand affect whether you rushed frantically to the store to get the last bottle of water because of a weather report warning of a drought.

Universal laws govern us whether we are aware of them are not. A farmer must know the laws of crop growth to be successful. An apple seed has a specific germination phase, need for certain lighting, water, and nutrients. A farmer must know all these variables in order to produce constant excellent produce. Imagine if a farmer randomly scattered a few different variety of seeds at the same time in the same area. Then the farmer threw some dirt on the seeds and, afterward, went about rejoicing in anticipation of a great harvest. How silly does this seem, but how often do we do the same thing? We scatter our thoughts, dreams or visions randomly and believe we will get a great harvest. We have great, lofty visions but never take the time to do the daily activities that are needed for those things to take root.

I believe there is a law of manifestation. This law governs how things move from the unseen world, or realm, to the seen. Stephen Covey states this best in his book "The Seven Habits of Highly Effective People." He states that creation happens twice: first in the mind and then in the physical world. The laws that govern creation seem to have a certain pattern. There appears to be a specific timeframe for each thing of its kind. For instance, a human baby typically takes nine months to go from almost invisible to visible in the external world. We know this as the birthing process. All animals and plants behave the same way. Imagine if I use the laws for an apple when planting an oak tree. I would always fail and remain in a state of constant frustration. First of all, I would never meet my expectations. My end product would never be what I expected. It's not very difficult to look at an acorn and believe it can and will become a mighty oak. This is because we are familiar with the process of its growth. No one stands over the tree and worries or frets thinking, "What if the birds never sit on its branches or what if it's too cold this winter for my poor trees?" This sounds insane, right? So why do we have difficulty believing that we, who contain the seeds of greatness within us, can grow to be as wonderful as the mighty oak? We need to see ourselves as the mighty oak even though we can only see the acorn potential.

We are hardwired for greatness but somehow we have forgotten and therefore got stuck looking at the acorn phase. As long as we focus on what we see we only see what we focus on. This is why I stress with much emphasis the following. It is imperative that you choose to begin re-scripting your life by envisioning yourself in your full bloom, also known as the "oak phase." Yes, the great mighty oak that we are called to be. God sees the end from the beginning, and this is the formula for greatness. The blueprint for success is seeing the full blossom of the matured tree while looking at the seed before it's even planted.

## Good and Evil

Growing up in a Christian household, I was raised on the story of Adam and Eve in the Garden of Eden. I still had lots of unanswered questions, though. Recently, I read *"The Four Agreements"* by Don Miguel Ruiz and found wonderful clarity. The belief is that as long as we avoid the tree of good and evil, all will be well. Perhaps, the tree of good and evil represents the duality of God or good. When I began to see good and bad because I didn't abide by the laws of my garden, I missed the mark, or sinned. This resulted in me developing the notion that I'm separated from the source of my garden when I sin. That thought keeps me feeling guilty and longing for something better. There are many versions of this belief system about good and evil. My purpose is not to convince you to believe in mine, but to encourage you to search your soul to find your own peace.

*As long as we focus on what we see, we only see what we focus on.*

I believe that the kingdom of God is within all of us, just like that mighty acorn. Wherever the kingdom is, there resides the King. So I personally believe God is not to be sought after out there, but it is an experience we awaken within us. My belief system says that Jesus, the Christ, died for my sins due to my missing the mark. He died so that I could return to my garden of Eden where I'm whole and perfect with everything that I need.

## In the Eye of the Beholder

God is like the air we breathe or the ocean in which the fish swim. There is no beginning and no end in Him. Since I am part of the whole, my individual cells or electrons act like me at any given time. Nobel prizewinning physicist Richard Feynman's double-slit thought experiment showed that an electron can act like either a particle or wave based on the opening (one slit or two slits) through which it passes. For practical purposes, we'll compare the varying slits to people observing the electron. Thus, the experiment shows that an electron behaves differently based on the observer. It's important to realize the significance of the possibilities here. If electrons, which are the energy form at our foundation, act this way, then the whole person must behave possible in the same manner. If we believe we are made in God's image and that God allows for the possibility of all things, then we, like our electrons, are also capable of all manner of possible outcomes. It all depends on how we look at the possibilities (electrons), however. Thus, there are multiple outcomes as well as multiple possibilities based on the observer of the electron. There are times when the electron acts like a particle and times when it acts like wave. There times when it acts like both, and instances when it acts like neither. All of these possibilities are based on who is observing the electron. Since on the energy level, we are electrons, then we too must possible behave the same way.

So what is a question we could be asking ourselves at this point? For one, who is observing our lives? From the view that we are born spiritual beings experiencing a human or physical life, then perhaps the observer is a spiritual being who sees endless possibilities without being limited by natural parameters. In any case, it's important to realize that we can be anything we want, but we have to believe it's possible. That may mean changing our outlook, the laws that govern our daily lives.

We accept laws for ourselves and govern our lives accordingly. Recently, I was in a conference in Canada. During one of the breaks, I decided to get a cup of tea when a young lady walked up to me and looked at the tea selection with frustration and stated, "The tea I want is always gone when I get here." I smiled because I had just been thinking the opposite for myself. The tea I want is always here when I need it. How funny how we both had accepted laws for ourselves around simple things such as a cup of tea.

I met her afterward and felt comfortable sharing that she had accepted this version of the law for herself, and it would always be true until she changed it. I encouraged her to begin stating that the tea she desires is always waiting for her to enjoy. She looked at me with amazement as if a light bulb had just gone off and smiled. She immediately repeated what I said, and to both our amazement, the kitchen staff refilled the teas while we were standing there. We couldn't help but laugh at how immediate her spoken words revealed a simple law in her life. As simple as this may sound, it is profound. I have stories and stories and testimonies after testimonies of similar instances.

So many people begin to instantaneously change their lives by changing how they relate to the laws that govern their lives. I have a patient who is a middle-aged white female who just couldn't seem to get her blood sugar, or diabetes, and therefore, foot pain under control. She had severe peripheral neuropathy, which is damage to the nerves caused by her blood sugar being high for a long period. I gave her a simple, take-home re-scription assignment. I told her to find out what was causing her to be so angry and bitter, and then work on changing it. She was shocked at my answer. She went on and on about how her husband did not do what he needed to do, resulting in her being in her current health condition. I told her to rise above the situation and see life from his perspective and then work on improving herself. She returned to the office one month later stating that once she rose above the situation, which had caused her to be upset and bent out of shape, her husband seemed to miraculously change overnight. In fact, he was more loving and compassionate to her. She said this lasted about a week until she slid back (backslid) into her old ways. When she did, she said he also returned to his old ways. She operated in the law of victim versus victor. The law of victim says someone is always causing harm to me, and I am a victim of my circumstance or others.

The patient soon realized that her continued physical sickness of uncontrolled Type 2 diabetes has its origin in her mind and how she was perceiving herself as a victim. (My book *"Diabetes Shouldn't Cost You an Arm or a Leg"* looks at the emotional and financial burden diabetes places on our nation, the individual and the family. She also realized that taking responsibility for her choices led to instantaneous happiness with less emotional turmoil. She never once had to beg or manipulate her husband to do better. She is the only one who changed. She made a choice to rise above the situation in which she saw herself as a victim, and she chose to see the stressful situation from her husband's perspective. In her own words, the results were "pretty miraculous." She said, "My husband became so kind and caring, and we really enjoyed each other's presence." That seemingly miraculous situation was maintained as long as she stayed above the situation where she could have a better perspective.

Ask yourself the following question: *What are some laws that I have accepted in my life that don't support me or serve me well?*

i.e. I can never get ahead. I've always the last to… I am never going to have enough money. My children will never amount to much.

*What are some laws that support you?* If you can't think of any, take this time to redefine or establish some new ones. Remember, it's your life, write what you want.

Examples of supportive laws include: I always have loving, supportive people and relationships in my life. I give and accept love daily. I am in a constant state of financial abundance every day.

## Purpose and Power

I have never seen this written, but I believe there is an unspoken law of purpose. What do I mean by this? I find that when people have purpose or a reason to live, they tend to be more happy and fulfilled. When a car is driven and well cared for, it tends to have a longer life. The longer it sits, the more its parts begin to rust and become nonfunctional. This is also seen in human beings. Over the years in my practice, I've seen thousands of people who have retired. Unfortunately, I've also noticed a pattern. Within 3 to 5 months of retiring, I usually hear bad news from the family of the individual. I typically get reports of everything from strokes to heart attacks to death. The individuals who are successful once they retire typically have a role or function that they enjoy doing and do every day. The people who retire to their couches to catch up on the long-needed rest they avoided during their work phase are usually the ones who experience rapid onset of disease, premature death, heart attacks, and strokes.

I've also seen a pattern among my older patients. The ones who are mobile and youthful tend to be involved in support groups such as yoga, dancing, swimming and religious organization. They also practice prayer and or meditation. On the contrary, the opposite is also observed. The patients who more readily develop dementia and chronic foot problems typically have little to no involvement in support groups or activities. They also tend to have less interaction with their families.

So what does this have to do with purpose? People with purpose and a reason to live tend to be happier, healthier and well-balanced. They also tend to be proactive in seeking podiatric care whereas the latter group tends to be more reactive. Reactivity leads to lengthy hospitalizations because of delayed medical intervention. One of my favorite saying is "an ounce of prevention is better than a pound of cure." I say this often because I see the devastation that delayed medical treatment has on the individual, the family, our society and even our economy. Type 2 diabetes is one of the leading causes of death, and unfortunately, most foot conditions are neglected, requiring below-the-knee or foot amputations. As a surgeon who performs amputations, I say the following with much passion and force. The responsibility must remain with the patient. I've found that patients who take ownership of their health tend to be more successful and are more often proactive versus reactive in their treatment, as well as seeking diagnosis.

As long as there is someone else to blame, than the power is out of your hands. If we blame the devil, the power is out of our hands. If we blame our doctor, the power is out of our hands. If we blame our spouse, the power is out of our hands. We blame our children. We blame our parents. We blame the government. However, whether we accept it or not, the power rests in our hands to maintain autonomy and control over our lives. We must take responsibility for the things that we can legitimately control and release those that we can't. The prayer of serenity says exactly that:

*"God, grant me the serenity to accept the things I cannot change, the courage to change the things I can, and the wisdom to know the difference."*

If you want to be happy, make inner peace a priority in your life. Create your own laws, such as, "I live in a state of constant peace regardless of my circumstance."

> *"God, grant me the serenity to accept the things I cannot change, the courage to change the things I can, and the wisdom to know the difference."*
>
> **~Reinhold Niebuhr**

Laws are constant and absolute. It matters not what type of person, their age, their sexual orientation or religious creed; the laws act the same at all times. The variables in the equation won't change. The laws act the same in Japan as they would in Jamaica. This is why it's said that it rains on the just and the unjust (Matt. 5:45). Rain doesn't see good or bad. It just does its thing; it rains.

We are governed by the laws of the universe in addition to the laws that we create for ourselves. Being aware of these laws helps us to play the key role in re-scripting our lives and walking into our divine destiny. In chapter 3, I'll discuss the power of systems. You'll begin to see the relationship between laws and systems. As a preview, think of systems as routes that you take on a highway to get to certain destinations. You have a route to your job, a route to your place of worship, and a route to go shopping. Those are your systems. You follow that route to achieve the desired outcome or get to a destination. Laws affect how you progress along the system or how your system breaks down.

As you begin to re-script your life, you must begin where you want to end, accept the associated laws, and create systems of success that are filled with constructive, not destructive, personal choices.

# Chapter 2 Written Exercise

1. Sit quietly in a room where you will be uninterrupted for at least 30 minutes.
2. Write seven laws that affect your life every day. Examples include laws of electricity, physics and gravity to name a few. Include how these laws affect your daily existence.

Law 1 _____

_____

Law 2 _____

_____

Law 3 _____

_____

Law 4 _____

_____

Law 5 _____

_____

Law 6 _____

_____

Law 7 _____

_____

3. List some laws that you would like to create for your life.

Examples of this include the following: I have loving and supportive relationships in my life; I am financially free, and my money works for me every day; Every cell in my body functions at its peak potential naturally; My children are people of excellence; and I make a difference in the lives of others every day.

1. _____
2. _____
3. _____
4. _____
5. _____
6. _____
7. _____
8. _____
9. _____
10. _____

In chapter 10, we will go into significant detail on putting the new laws the you create into motion. Your job right now is simply to write the things that you desire in your life. Again, remember it's important to be as specific as possible. The more vague you write your desires, the more vague your results will be. Use your words as if they were the bricks to a beautiful house that you are building. So, make every one matter. It's the worst feeling to assemble something only to find extra parts or screws left out. Your mind is never truly at ease since you're wondering what step was missed or how potentially unstable your project will be. Therefore, use your words and the exactness of them to be as specific as possible.

While completing my surgical residency at New York Methodist hospital in Brooklyn, we were told over and over to make every incision matter. When you're making an incision with a scalpel on a patient, every single incision must have a purpose. So now I'm instructing you to do the same. Write your vision. Make every word matter.

Envision that your words are the building blocks of your life. The more detailed your words, the more detailed and magnificent your life. Imagine if every word you wrote and then spoke took a life form and appeared in front of you. What would you then speak? What then would you write? I challenge you to believe that you have the power of both writing and speaking your life into existence. Whether you believe it or not, you're already doing it.

I remember when I met my husband in undergrad at Oral Roberts University. Within two weeks of dating, we were walking to dinner and I ran up the steps to the dining commons ahead of him. Right as I got to the top of the stairs, I turned around and jokingly said, "you know, I'll probably end up marrying you". And I just turned around and kept running up the steps without even thinking anything of it. That's exactly what happened, but understand, it didn't happen immediately. Remember, we dated for seven years. I actually had to give him an ultimatum at 6 ½ years since I figured that was more than sufficient time for him to make up his mind. After all, look at what he was getting. Could the decision really be that hard? Tooting my own horn here!

Growing up, my dad would always say, "No idle jesting." That basically meant don't use words without a purpose. As a result, my words had always been gold to me. What I said meant everything. I knew the power of my words even when I was joking, so I always carefully chose all my words. My dad had created this law in our household, and therefore, we governed ourselves around it. No idle jesting was one of his 10 Commandments. I've loosened up quite a bit since those days, but nevertheless, the principle remains the same with me. We create and utilize laws to function in our daily lives. Be astute to your role.

# 3

# THE POWER OF SYSTEMS

Before we talk about choices, we must first examine the power of systems. Systems allow the proper order, communication, and function. For permanent change to occur, there must be the development of supportive systems, which are governed by our supportive laws. These supportive systems are important since they are like the foundation.

The best examples of systems within our bodies are the organ systems. Our circulatory system works fairly effortlessly without us ever having to think about it. For instance, I don't have to think to allow my heart to beat. We never even have to wonder how a pacemaker is doing to keep the heart going at the right rate. These things happen automatically. These are built-in systems that only need to be maintained. They are automatically established at birth. Our role in maintaining the integrity of these systems is keeping our bodies healthy.

Every major organ system is built up by a smaller cellular system. On the cellular level, each cell functions in its own world and in the world around it. A cellular protein called laminin is seen as the foundation or basement membrane. It is called the rebar, or glue, of our bodies. Laminin is a cellular adhesive molecule and tells each cell what its role will be in the body. Basically, it's the director of the system. It tells each cell what its role will be when it becomes big or an organ. Systems are vital because without them, chaos happens. When the laminin is altered in the body or missing cancers are seen.

Our respiratory system is also automatic although we can choose to take a deep or shallow breath. However, we don't have to tell our lungs to keep breathing. It just happens. Good personal systems

*Success is not a secret, it's a system.*

*~ Florence Scovel Shinn*

function the same way. They are as automatic as they can be and only require routine maintenance to continue to function.

One of my favorite authors Florence Scovel Shinn, the author of *"The Game of Life and How to Play It,"* says "Success is not a secret; it's a system." When I first heard those words, light bulbs came on in my head. It made so much sense. I began to look at companies that are successful. McDonald's, for instance, has had systems in place that has brought them tremendous success. McDonald's University teaches every franchise owner the systems of how to run a successful McDonald's restaurant. It doesn't matter where it is located, McDonald's delivers the same product across the board consistently.

I met with a colleague who runs one of the most successful podiatry practices, and at the end of our meeting, he turned to me and said, "Suzette, it's not people who fail, it's people without systems who fail." Again, I was hearing this "S" word again: systems, systems, systems. Thus, I began to look at my life to see what systems I had in place and where I could implement systems to do better. I looked to see if I had systems that needed updating or just needed to be discarded. As I began doing this, I realized that I could decrease my effort and increase excellence and productivity. I began incorporating systems that were more productive in my home life and found that things ran a lot more smoothly without so much rush, confusion or yelling. I realize I wasn't a bad person, I only had poor or no good systems in place. I believed in this so much that I created the following saying: "Health is not a secret, it's a system of healthy habits." The more I said this, the more it made sense to me. I realized how true it was when patients began to overcome their Type 2 diabetes, high blood pressure and high cholesterol by losing weight and incorporating healthier eating plans. I recommended that they learn how to pray and meditate, increase their movement, and eat natural foods, avoiding processed foods. I even recommended that some go to food addicts anonymous. Without fail, the ones who embraced incorporation of these healthy recommendations have all seen dramatic results in their lives. Once their weight approached normal, their need for excessive medications either decreased or totally dissipated. Some patients have established normal blood sugar or blood pressure in less than a month after eating, moving and thinking in a healthy manner.

# Interdependence

As an individual, I am made up of an array of systems. There are systems that allow my body to function, and likewise, I am a part of my family and work systems. Just like each organ has its specific function, so does each role I have in my family and work. My role as a wife, mother, sister, boss, colleague, and friend all have distinctly different functions.

The circulatory system works in unison with the respiratory system, which fully respects the excretory system and so on. All aspects of the systems have distinct functions or purposes, but they work to benefit the whole. When there is a break or breach in any of the systems, that part begins to show dysfunction or disease and may eventually cause the whole to die. The arteries bring blood and oxygen away from the heart, and the vein returns deoxygenated blood to the heart. Since the primary role of the arteries is to deliver oxygen and nutrients to the organs and the body, imagine what happens when the heart is malfunctioning. When an artery is blocked or narrowed, it is unable to deliver its life-giving oxygen and nutrients to the area beyond it, also known as distal to the blockage, and that area begins to die. This is the definition of gangrene. Gangrene is loss of oxygen to the tissue, so the tissue dies. Can the body live without oxygen? No, this is why emergency treatment of conditions such as heart attacks

> *Health is not a secret; it's a system of healthy habits.*
>
> *~ Suzette Clements*

or strokes is so key. The outcome of the individual is directly related to immediate intervention to restore the proper system of blood flow.

Communication is a system we often overlook. It is a vital system that must be maintained regularly. The cells in our bodies communicate with each other via cell walls and membranes. These membranes are very specific as to what is allowed to enter or exit the cell. There are proteins, such as cholesterol, that are necessary parts of the membrane that allow for normal function and communication between the cells. Too much cholesterol can lead to accumulation of plaque in the artery walls leading to blockage and often gangrene.

In a relationship, proper communication is a must for functioning and living a happy life. Relationships based on assumptions tend to be unhappy and or short-lived. Relationships with frequent, open and honest communication tend to be long-lasting.

In nature, we see the effects of communication between animals in the wild. Even animals have their own form of communication to keep their young safe from predators. When these rules are not adhered to, we often see the untimely death of the new offspring because it strayed from its zone of safety. When my husband and I were newlyweds, we often argued because of miscommunication. I said one thing, but he heard another or vice versa. I was the queen of poor communication. I expected him to read my mind. After all, he and I had dated for seven years, so he should have known what I wanted by then. I would cause my own heartache by holding my feelings or words in for weeks and then erupting like a volcano. I can laugh about it now, but it was not pretty at the time. As we matured, the communication lines improved in our relationship and our marriage blossomed.

## Maintenance

Systems also require management and maintenance. A healthy body easily becomes diseased when it is poorly maintained. As mentioned, high cholesterol soon becomes plaque along the walls of the arteries leading to peripheral arterial disease also known as PAD. Similarly, the yard becomes overgrown without lawn care on a regular basis. A flower garden develops weeds and unwanted bugs from neglect. In general, out of balance systems show disease (Dis-ease), or dysfunction.

Healthy Artery

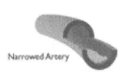

Narrowed Artery

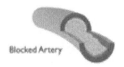

Blocked Artery

The picture is a comparison of a cross section of an artery. The top image is a healthy artery that is open without excessive plaque, which allows for open healthy blood flow. The middle shows a narrowed arterial vessel which represents decreased blood flow resulting in decreased oxygen to any part beyond the narrowing. The blocked artery shown at the bottom results in death to the tissue beyond the blockage. This is known as gangrene. The latter two represents systems out of balance due to lack of systems of maintenance.

Most people understand the principle of maintenance for their car; however, most people have no maintenance of the body. They have a routine maintenance for changing the oil, rotating their tires and getting tune-ups. The care typically comes from a manual that gives the intervals of recommended maintenance. We know that if we drive for too long without changing or adding oil, the engine will be destroyed. I know this firsthand.

In college, I drove a little blue Honda Civic, which was my first car. It held a lot of significance since my older sister, Regna, gave it to me. It was her first car and that meant a tremendous amount to us. I treated it like gold. I had regular tune-ups, and oil changes were done every 3,500 miles as recommended. It was great on gas and would fit up to five people somewhat comfortably if we all took turns breathing (laugh out loud). Well, one summer, a friend asked if she could borrow my car since I would not be using it while on my missions trip to Mexico. I agreed, assuming she would care for it like my sister and I had. At the end of the summer, on my way home from the airport, I saw my baby blue Honda Civic on the side of the highway in Tulsa, Oklahoma. I immediately called her to find out why it was there. After many unsuccessful attempts to get her, she finally returned my call. She drove the car without oil and blew the engine. Yes, my baby that had been so faithful had died on the side of the road. She accepted no responsibility, and since the car was old, I decided that fixing it would cost more than it was worth.

I gained several valuable lessons from this experience.

For systems to flow, there must be proper communication and no assumptions. I assume she would change the oil if or when the oil light came on. I also realize that vital parts of the system should never be taken out of place. What do I mean by that? I should've said no when she asked to use the car. My car represented my ability to do my clinical rotations at the various hospitals, and now I was without transportation in Tulsa. My independent system of transportation was now altered. The third lesson I learned was that although this was a bad situation, a good result could come from it. A few months later, I bought my first brand-new car, a burgundy Volkswagen Jetta. It was much more reliable, and everything worked out for my best in the end.

# Chapter 3 Written Assignment

1. Sit quietly and take three deep breaths.
2. List three systems in which you could use some improvement, including communication, relationship, health, organization, finances, etc.

   a. _____

   b. _____

   c. _____

3. List three systems in your life in which you have success and want to reinforce.

   a. _____

   b. _____

   c. _____

4. List five unsupportive systems that you would like to replace in your life.

   1. _____

      _____

   2. _____

      _____

   3. _____

      _____

   4. _____

      _____

5. _____

_____

5. List five new support systems you want to incorporate to replace the five unsupportive systems above.

1. _____

_____

2. _____

_____

3. _____

_____

4. _____

_____

5. _____

_____

6. Where would you like to see yourself in the systems one year from now.

7. What is just one thing you could begin doing daily/ weekly/monthly to make it happen.

8. Now, ask yourself, "What do or can I do on a daily, weekly, monthly or yearly basis to have success in the systems?"

When I was in nursing school at ORU, I had the pleasure of being the student of Kenda Jezek. She was one of my clinical instructors at the time, and she is now the dean of the school of nursing. I remember as if it were yesterday. We were all anxious and feeling overwhelmed with the course curriculum, but she gave the best analogy of how to tackle the task of becoming an excellent nurse. She asked, "How do you eat an elephant?"

All of our answers varied. With my Jamaican accent, I joked, "Well, I'd chop it up and put some jerk sauce on it."

Her answer was simply, "One bite at a time."

This answer was so simple, yet so profound to me. I've used this analogy since my 20s and have always had success with it.

So my question to you today is the same if you look at re-scripting your life as seemingly insurmountable, the proverbial elephant. Know that it's possible to eat this elephant one bite at a time when you take small steps in the direction of your desired goal and outcome. Don't become overwhelmed. Others have done this, and you can do this with ease and little effort. Notice the words I use here. Remember, your words are powerful. If you believe it's too difficult and the task improbable, then that will become your reality and your truth. So begin re-scripting by using words such as, "It will happen with ease and effortlessly. I will enjoy every step of the way. I will have loving supportive people along my journey." All of these words are constructive and become your truth. The more you say them, the more you see that they bring your truth into this realm.

In chapter 6 the power of habits will be introduced. Habits are vital and powerful since they are like the bricks that build a mansion, no matter how big your dreams are. Every single brick or habit is crucial. In chapter 12, we will discuss in detail how to put it all together, including the power of the tongue to create and produce life or death.

# 4

# THE POWER OF CHOICES

As human beings, we have an amazing thing called choice. Webster's defines choice as the act of choosing. Our perception of whether we have choices or not depends on our belief system, however. We are generally picking or deciding between two or more possibilities. Choice redefined is then the act of deciding between two or more possibilities.

The best part of being a human being is our ability to make choices. An acorn can't decide that it wants to grow in England instead of the U.S. and just pick up and move. What does this all have to do with scripting my life? Choices are like the tires on a car, which is the foundational part of the transportation system that take you to your desired destination. Without proper tires, your foundation will collapse, and you won't move forward.

Without making proper choices, you may want to see change, but it never manifests. Choices help us move from one location to another. It is said if you want to see how an

> *Choice Re-defined:*
> *The conscious act of deciding between two or more possibilities*
>
> *~ Suzette Clements*

individual will be five years from now, look at his daily habits. In chapter 6, we will discuss how habits affect our journey towards our destination. Choices are key if we want to move in a forward direction. Bad choices either keep us stagnant or move us backward.

# What to Choose

The feet are your foundation, and if the foundation is altered, then everything in the superstructure becomes altered. I say this because I find patients who will take medications to treat the symptom while ignoring the true problem. For instance, if a patient comes in with heel pain caused by excessive flattening of the arch, known as pronation, I can give an injection that will decrease the inflammation around the soft tissue. However, this is only treating the symptom. I must also place the patient in an orthotic device to limit the rolling in of the arch to actually treat the problem. If patients wait too long before getting treatment, they will also have the same problem on the opposite foot. This is often because they are compensating. When one side hurts, they try to avoid pain, so it begins putting excessive weight on the other side, or the contra lateral limb. My goal is to get the person walking normally, putting equal weight on both feet as soon as possible. Sometimes the pain becomes so intense that it may cause ankle injuries or even knee injuries. If the heel pain is severe, the patient may even walk on their toes and cause pinching of the nerve between the long bones of the foot and even stress fractures.

In life, it's always best to look at solving the problem versus treating a symptom. Treating a symptom will only give temporary relief and guarantee a return of the problem. It's the same principle as driving with bald tires and never aligning the car. Both are important. The balding of the tire is usually because the car is misaligned. So one must both align the car and put new tires on to keep the car driving straight. I say all this to say that choices are like the tires on the vehicle that keeps us moving in the direction of our desired end. When the tires are deflated, the car has difficulty moving forward.

Poor choices can lead to blowouts, which can lead to accidents. Having a spare in the trunk is always a good practice since accidents may occur. Always have a plan(spare) of what to do in the event of unfortunate situations or in the event of an accident or tragedy. The point is that we must choose to be prepared to ensure we can keep moving forward. No matter what the roadblock, there's always a solution.

# How to Choose It

So now that you've decided to re-script your life, you may have asked yourself, where do I begin? Which aspect of my life do I tackle first? At first, it may feel a bit overwhelming, but don't lose heart. If you just stick to the plan, things will begin to lineup shortly thereafter. If you get a sick feeling in your stomach, look in the mirror directly into your own eyes and say: "If others can do it, then I can do it also." Say this every time you get this nervous feeling.

How you choose where to begin depends on your personality type. If you are a person who is very disciplined and works well in systems, this will be a simple process for you. If you are a procrastinator and feel as if you lack discipline, then you will do best to start with the task you believe is most difficult. Since your nature is typically to avoid these things, you must schedule your most difficult task to be completed first.

Having difficulty focusing is common at first. Write down how you plan on rewarding yourself once you complete these tasks. The more you do this, the easier

> "If others can do it, then I can do it also."

it will become. You will begin doing more difficult tasks with less dread and procrastination. By choosing to do the most difficult task first, you will soon notice your ability to focus and organize will improve. Begin using words such as, "I am disciplined" or "I choose to be disciplined." Say them even before you become what you are saying. Remember, you are deciding between two or more possibilities.

When you begin making these declarations, act as if you already have the thing you are declaring. Examine people you know who are very disciplined. Ask yourself what are some things they have in common? Typically, they have the ability to delay their gratification by self-control, and they tend to avoid unhealthy excesses.

# Choosing Your State of Mind

While I was in podiatry school, we lived in a small four-bedroom brick home that I purchased at age 23 after graduating from nursing school. In 2002, after completing my surgical residency in podiatry in New York, my family and I relocated back to Georgia. When we originally left for New York, our son Kirby III was 18 months old. When we returned to Georgia, we had another addition to our family. Our daughter, Gabrielle, who was born in 2000 in Brooklyn, New York, and was 18 months when we moved back to Georgia.

The house was in an older neighborhood, but we wanted a new or newer home in which to raise our children. Although we made several trips in the latter parts of my residency attempting to find a new home, it was difficult shopping for homes while in New York. Despite our best efforts, we were unable to purchase a new home in Georgia while still living in New York. Therefore, when we relocated to Georgia, we moved back into our original home despite our reservations about its small size and dated style. We resolved to do what I said earlier. We decided to be happy in that house. We made a conscious CHOICE to bloom where we were planted.

We went to the paint store and began fixing up the little house. I love to paint flowers, so I painted a beautiful flower garden mural in the hallway leading to the kids' rooms. Every time I saw the flowers, I felt very warm and happy in our home. Within less than a week of completing my masterpiece mural, a lady from Emory University offered to buy our little home for cash. We closed on that house on a Wednesday and moved into our brand-new home the next day. The new home was exactly what we were looking for. It was nothing short of miraculous. With the money from the sale of the house, we were able to start both of our practices, pay off some loans, furnish our new home, and get settled. It would've been so easy to complain because we were tired from the big move from New York to Georgia, but we did not. We chose to be happy right where we were.

Happiness is an art that is best obtained by living in the moment. Once we decided to be happy where we were, doors began to open in our favor. These doors opened almost effortlessly.

Are you working hard to make things happen without any evidence of progress? If you answered yes, ask yourself: How would I feel if I had all the things I desired? How would I feel if I had a new house, a smart child, a loving spouse, a stylish car, a promising career, or a fit body? Would I be happy then?

Have you ever wondered why some people just always seem to walk around with a cloud over their heads? Do you know anyone who always has something bad to say about everything and everyone? We all do. The opposite scenario is also objectionable. Some people seem like the sun is always shining on them, and they also tend to find something good to say about others no matter what. Just as being a victim is a choice, happiness is a choice. I'm not saying anyone who is a victim chooses to be a victim, what I am saying is that the victim mentality is a choice.

I have been in patient care since age 16 in some form or another. I have worked in nursing homes, hospitals, personal-care homes, surgical centers, as well as my private practice. That's over 31 years of observing and asking questions of my patients. In three decades, I have observed victims of circumstances who became victorious and were inspirational and encouraging to me as well as those around them.

Have you ever called someone to encourage them and they encouraged you? I remember when my brother-in-law Dave was diagnosed with Hodgkin's lymphoma and undergoing treatment. I called him and his words and attitudes were so positive that he ended up encouraging me instead of me encouraging him. He is a perfect example of your attitude determines your altitude. Within a short period of time and until today he has been in remission and looks better than ever. He also improved his eating habits and ultimately became a vegan. However, due to his sickness, no one would hire him for some time. He is now happily working and has been for over 7 years.

Throughout the years, I noticed that people with the most diseases, medications and allergies were most often much less pleasant than those who were disease or medication free. There are some exceptions, but for the most part, this has been my consistent observation. The ones who had a pleasant demeanor or positive outlook on life tended to have less chronic illnesses and pain. They often responded to my treatment approximately 50% faster as well. They also tended to be confident and secure in themselves and very appreciative of my care. These people seemed to carry sunshine with them. I would describe them as having a victorious mentality. This is not to say that they did not have problems. In fact, they often did, but the problem didn't have them.

In my last seven years of practice, I've also noticed a trend in patients with Type 2 diabetes. Some being treated with insulin and tablets to decrease their blood sugar, become medication free as a result of learning how to eat, think and move properly. It's important to note that these patients worked with their primary care physicians as well as their other doctors and/or caretakers to incorporate a more healthy diet and active lifestyle. In my book *"Get Your Mind Right and Your Body Will Follow,"* I discuss the dangers of bad thinking on the body along with producing lifestyle diseases and how to reverse them. Whether you see yourself as a victim or victor, you are right.

# Chapter 4 Written Exercise

1.  Sit quietly and take three deep breaths.

2.  Ask yourself, do I see myself as a victim or victorious?

3.  Did you answer victim? Do this simple experiment. For the next 24 hours practice saying the opposite of what you are programmed to say. This makes you accountable for your words until it becomes a habit. Practice, practice, practice. Initially it may feel uncomfortable. Push beyond this feeling. Remember, if other people can do it, you can do it also. Begin to listen to how other people speak. Don't judge, just listen.

4.  Start with one desired outcome. Close your eyes and imagine yourself having it. If it's a new house, see yourself opening the door and walking in. Observe every little detail of the home. Notice the colors on the wall, the specific accents on the staircase, the lighting and the sun shining through the kitchen window. Open the patio door and inhale a big breath of fresh air. Can you smell the fresh cut grass? As kids, we had beautiful imaginations and somehow allowed life to steal this beautiful process of co-creating. Repeat this envisioning at least daily, preferably twice a day early in the morning upon waking and at bedtime before drifting off.

There is power in numbers. I find the kids are natural visionaries and help bring artistic imaginations to life. My husband, who is the left brain/logical one, found it very difficult at first to imagine with me, but with practice, it became easier for him. I didn't say easy; I said easier. I also invited our children in on the process, and they were naturals. They jumped right in and had no problem stating what they wanted and how they felt once they received what they wanted. So if you have children in your life or other significant others, allow them to become a part of this because whether you realize it or not, they will become part of your vision at some point. Allow them to be a significant part of the co-creation. You can either plan for it and proactively walk into it or just allow it to happen based on life circumstances. Be creative here and have fun. I find the more we are scripted, the more difficult it appears at first. Lose your social and emotional barriers and become like a little child, carefree and inquisitive.

5.   Sometimes things happen so fast you forget and don't see your part in bringing them to fruition. So, stay alert and write things down as they come to pass. Keep a journal at your bedside. Sidebar here: Always begin your journal with something you are thankful for. Oprah calls it a gratitude journal. Same concept here. In my old Pentecostal church back home in Jamaica, they would say, "You can't out give God." The point I'm making is, be thankful. Write the things that you are thankful for every day. Do this until it becomes a habit.

In Matthew 25:14-30, Jesus shared the parable of the talents. All three were given talents of money, but one hid his. The other two used theirs wisely and allowed it to increase. Gratitude is like a talent in that it only grows when shared or given away. Get into the habit of giving and sharing gratitude easily and effortlessly. Choose to be a thankful person. It is often overlooked that the one who did not multiply his talents did not get an increase. As a matter of fact, it was taken from him. The ones who had an increase were rewarded above and beyond that which they had.

Neville Goddard, the author of *Feeling is the Secret*, recommends the above process twice a day. He states that, while in the state akin to sleep, envision yourself in possession of your dream or desired outcome. The state should be felt as if it were already attained. In the Scriptures, we are taught to speak the things that aren't as though they were (Rom. 14:7). We are also taught that when we pray, we should believe that we are receiving the thing that we're praying for at the time of prayer. Nowhere does it say that you wait until you get the thing that you're praying for to believe. This would not require faith.

Faith is the ladder between the desire and the manifestation. Faith requires stepping in the direction of your desired outcome. Wanting it is not enough. You must take the required steps of faith. This is why it's important to begin speaking the things that aren't as though they were. You're not lying. You are basically becoming your own prophetic voice. You speak it into manifesting in your own life. Begin speaking your desired outcome as though it occurred.

# 5

# THE POWER OF
# OUR BELIEF SYSTEM

## Who told you that?

From the day we are born, we begin the creation of our belief system. We are the products of our habits, thoughts and deeds. As children, we are influenced by our environment, teachers, religious leaders, siblings, friends, and caregivers. For the purpose of this book, I will only focus on external influences and not the genetic ones. My goal is to help you identify the things in your life that you have power and control over. This is what the serenity prayer espouses. As stated earlier it states, "God, grant me the serenity to accept the things I cannot change, the courage to change the things I can, and the wisdom to know the difference."

If you don't think our belief systems alter our life in a significant manner, consider how differently we all respond to similar events. Two kids were playing at the park. Suddenly a dog ran up to the children. The first child was deathly afraid of dogs and ran to his mom who was equally afraid. She loudly instructed her son to run from the "bad, scary dog." Meanwhile, the second child stood quietly and talked to the dog's owner while his mom watched calmly. With permission of the dog owner, the second child was able to pet the dog and found him to be calm and playful.

# External Influences

The influences from external sources mold us into who we are. I grew up in the beautiful countryside of Jamaica and remember many stories and experiences specific to that region. These stories created the foundation of my core belief system. At age 8, we relocated to Cincinnati, Ohio, which immediately began to challenge many of the things I had come to know as true. You see, in our neighborhood back in Jamaica, my parents' voice and words carried significant authority. My dad was a Pentecostal preacher, and my mom was an evangelistic missionary. They were solid pillars in our community, and they lived and breathed their belief system. They truly walked the walk and talked the talk. This resulted in our home being a center of hope. At any given time, there was some form of counseling or inspiration being given to people seeking to improve the quality of their lives. Both my parents loved to help people and believed in doing it through the application of biblical principles. They practiced excellence and loved what they believed.

Relocating to a new country added new perspectives that began to challenge the core beliefs that I had been taught. One of my fun memories was playing with our neighbor's children. They had two girls who were one or two years younger than me and two older sons. One day while playing with my new best friend, Joy, I heard her mom call her to clean her room. An argument broke out between them. My friend ran to her room, slammed the door, and screamed, "I hate you mom." Those kinds of words, especially directed toward a parent, were not even on my hard drive of beliefs. I was shocked that anyone could let such destructive words out of their mouth. I sat speechless, but I knew my face said it all.

In my world, the only words I had been programmed to use to answer my parents were "yes" or "no" mommy or daddy. We often even addressed them as "sir" or "ma'am." Imagine the neurons that were firing in my brain at that point. I'd never seen this behavior before, not even the adults in my world talked like this. I saw the frustration on Joy and her mother's face. I did not believe it was my place to say anything, so I quietly went home.

The concept of dialogue versus monologue between a parent and child was born. I felt no need to change my communication with my parents since what we had seemed to work pretty well for us. However, some of my older siblings who were in high school began to challenge their core belief of respect due to exposure to their American peers. The peaceful home I had become accustomed to began changing drastically. Quite honestly, all hell broke loose. It seemed that my parents were no longer the only voice of authority in our home. This led to the onset of many communication outbreaks somewhat similar to the one my friend had with her mom. No one screamed, "I hate you, mom," but there was plenty of, "Well, I'm just gonna leave" or "It's my life. I want to live it my way," etc.

## Resetting Your System

Belief systems are formed by multiple internal and external factors. Some serve us for a lifetime while others are only for a season due to the conditions at that time. We are all on an ongoing quest to find our own path, and this mission is directly affected by our own belief system. Many influences will provide input, but we must carefully choose the ones that support us the best. The belief that kids should be seen and not heard was no longer serving and therefore was ultimately challenge.

We are somewhat like a computer, which is being programmed by our ideas and experiences. The hard drive represents our core processor or belief systems. Whatever is running in the background on the processor will manifest. Are there self-limiting beliefs running on your hard drive? Were you told by some kid in elementary school that you were ugly and you are still affected by that comment? Did a teacher or administrator ever tell you that you would never amount to anything? Did a parent label you is "no good"?

I want to challenge you to begin cleaning your belief system hardware, or hard drive. Go through your files and see what's on them. Some files were only four season, but we still have them running. These old corrupt files are leading to sluggish functioning. There are also some viruses in the form of negative belief systems that must be identified and deleted immediately. Unfortunately, you may still be holding onto these things. In the same way, a virus or too many programs running simultaneously can negatively affect the speed of the computer and limit its performance. The same thing often happens in our lives. Negative belief systems negatively affect our lives. If every time you begin moving in the direction of your desire, you recall negative messages from an unsupportive parent, a demeaning teacher or a relentless bully, then you may act as though their words still have power over you. Their voices only have the power you give them, though. It's time to re-script your core belief system and remove the viruses, Set up pop-up blockers for these negative voices and reboot your hard drive and your life.

Most people listen to messages, or voices, from people who have died. For instance, we do this when we read books. The Bible is comprised of accounts from people who have died but still impact us today. Our textbooks are mostly about dead people's opinions and experiences. A parent or friend may have meant well and somehow spoke or acted in a way that caused you offense. You may have resented what or how the person said something and still hold resentments today. Some of these voices are long since dead and gone, but we still give them the same power to influence us. In some cases, this is good, and in others, it is detrimental.

There are two affirmations that I found tremendously helpful on my journey to finding my true self. In the book

*"The Game of Life and How to Play It"* by Florence Scovel Shinn, she makes affirmations that I recommend using to begin cleaning your hard drive and installing your virus or spyware.

The affirmation for removal goes as follows:

"I now smash and demolish (by my spoken word) every untrue record in my subconscious mind. It shall return to the dust-heap of its native nothingness, for they came from my own vain imaginings. I now make perfect records through the Christ within – the records of health, wealth, love, and perfect self-expression. This is the square root of life, the game completed."

I use this affirmation frequently when old, untrue belief systems pop up in my head that no longer serve me. I found it to be very instrumental. Once I clean out my hard drive, I replace it with the following:

"Infinite Spirit, open the way for the Divine Design of my life to manifest; let the genius within me now be released; let me see clearly the perfect plan." The perfect plan includes health, wealth, love, and perfect self-expression.

After cleaning your hard drive of the unnatural, untrue or unfit, you must replace it with "something" positive. In this regard, Matthew 12:43-45 warns:

*"Now when the unclean spirit goes out of a man, it passes*

*through waterless places seeking rest, and does not find it. Then it says, 'I will return to my house from which I came.' And when it comes, it finds it unoccupied, swept, and put in order. Then it goes and takes along with it seven other spirits more wicked than itself, and they go in and live there; and the last state of that man becomes worse than the first..."*

Unclean spirits are basically anything that keeps us from seeing the perfection that God made us to be. For some people, this could be anger, fear, pride, jealousy, lust, gluttony, or so forth. Essentially, it's anything that would keep you from your divine design or assignment.

It's important to also note that you don't want to replace one bad habit with another bad habit. For example, people who stop smoking begin overeating and find themselves going from a chain smoker to a food addict. Once you clean the hard drive of these "unclean spirits," then you must reprogram and replace them with things such as love, integrity, and purity. Philippians 4:8 says, "Whatsoever things are true, honorable, right, pure, lovely, of good repute, if there is any excellence and anything worthy of praise, these

> *Infinite spirit, open the way for the divine design of my life to manifest; let the genius within me now be released. Let me see clearly the perfect plan. The perfect plan includes health, wealth, love and perfect self-expression.*
>
> *-Florence Scovel Shinn*

are the things we should think on." In Chapter 12, more practical ways will be given to implement this process.

# Finding You

It's important to realize that some things we were taught as children or in our early adulthood may no longer be applicable in this season of our life. In one community, for instance, a set of rules may have been applicable, but now, in a new community, they are no longer applicable and may even prove counterproductive. Therefore, search your heart and be true to yourself. Go within and ask questions. The answers are within you. Once you begin listening, you will actually hear a still small voice. That voice is your inner guidance. Your pilot light. All humans have it. It is intuition, also known as our instinctive feeling. We, in Christianity, call it the Holy Spirit. It is always running in the background. Unfortunately, the louder voices often drown it out.

Prayer and meditation are the two known ways to reconnect with the Divine within us. Prayer and meditation are to our spiritual life like our arteries and veins are to our bodies. Meditation carries similar properties to the arteries. The arteries bring oxygen away from the heart, if we see God as the heart. The veins bring deoxygenated blood back to the heart, somewhat like prayers. A body needs both arteries and veins to function at their peak potential. At no point do arteries believe they are better than veins. They don't ever declare, "We're going to work on our own." They are designed to work in a synchronized, harmonious manner. The same way meditation and prayer are in place to keep us in constant connection with our Divine. The blood carriers oxygen, and without oxygen, the tissue dies. This death of the tissue is also known as gangrene, which is loss of oxygen to the tissue, so the tissue dies. Spiritual gangrene is seen when we become disconnected from our source. I liken the spirit to the blood, which is the vehicle that carries the life. Like our blood carries oxygen, the Holy Spirit carries light. We, in our infinite forms, are light. Jesus said I am the light of the world. We are all also lights. Unfortunately, some of us only have a flicker of light and need to be rekindled.

Prayer petitions God. Meditation is the Divine design for spiritual renewal and keeps our internal light shining. It is the process of maintaining a spiritual fill up or tune up. We are avatars that house a beautiful Spirit, who is eternal. That spirit was never born and will never die. This is what makes us immortal, spiritual beings.

My dad died in 2007, and I went to the funeral home to view his body. I stared at the body that resembled an avatar, realizing that without the spirit of life, that body was not the beautiful father I knew. I then had an "Aha" moment. To be absent from the body is to be present with Christ (2 Cor. 5:8). That Scripture repeated in my head over and over and over. To be absent from the body, the avatar, is to be present with the Christ consciousness, or in spirit. The spiritual being, was not dead. He simply left his avatar behind. Once I had this revelation, I had an overwhelming sense of peace and comfort. The Scripture that I quoted so many times finally added meaning to me.

# Chapter 5 Written Exercise

1. Sit quietly where you not be interrupted for at least 20 minutes. Take three deep breaths and relax.

2. Affirm that "God makes no mistakes, and everything in my life, past and present, happened for a reason, and that reason is here to serve me." (Memorize and use it needed.)

3. Affirm that "Every man or woman along my path is a teacher."

4. If past voices still affect you negatively, learn to disarm them by saying the following: "They did their best with what they had at the time." No matter what the offense is, you can choose to release it right now. Ask yourself the following question: Do I want to be right, or do I want to be happy?

Remember that forgiveness is healing for the victim, the person who received the offense. There are also times when the offender will benefit from the act of forgiveness. Your job is to just forgive. Don't worry about what happens when you forgive or ask for forgiveness – even if the person is dead and long gone. Still forgive even if the other person was wrong. When we forgive others, we release bitterness that leads to our own healing. Similarly, asking for forgiveness relieves guilt that allows us to stop punishing ourselves or seeing ourselves as a bad person rather than a person who made a mistake. Remember, it's important to forgive ourselves too.

Write down a list of people you need to forgive or ask forgiveness. Include your own name if appropriate.

_____

_____

_____

_____

_____

_____

Plan the moment (date/time) and means (phone, letter, etc.) you will communicate your pardon or remorse. If the person died or moved away, you may need to forgive him/her through prayer.

What did you learn from each situation in which you need to forgive or ask for forgiveness?

_____

_____

_____

_____

_____

_____

5.  Add new supportive affirmations after deleting the old non-supportive ones. The Lord's Prayer is a perfect example. Forgive us our trespasses as we forgive those that trespass against us....

6.    Affirm that "I learn from all my mistakes and regard them as experiences and stepping stones."

Below is a "Re-Scription," like a medical prescription, it is a word I coined that means the purposeful use of productive words to heal and restore. They are affirmations with recommended usage just like a prescription. A Re-Scription for mistakes becomes an experience to learn and produce stepping stones to climb to your greater good.

---

# Rx for Happiness
*aka*
## Re-Scription

*"I learn from all my mistakes and regard them as experiences and stepping stones."*

*Sig: Take as needed for failure to move forward due to poor choices or regrets*

*Unlimited refills*

*Suzette Clements, DPM*

---

# 6

# THE POWER OF OUR HABITS

If choices are the tires of our system of success, then habits are the fuel that keeps the car running. A car can't run without fuel. Habits are the things we do by choice every day that govern our long-term outcome. They are the day in, day out results of our choices. A successful life must include successful habits. The two are inseparable.

Although habits are not automatic and can change, they are often established through much repetition and routine. We are creatures of comfort. We love to do the same thing over and over, the way we've always done it. When we are asked to change, it makes us feel uncomfortable because it takes us out our comfort zone. We define insanity as doing the same thing over and over and expecting a different result. If this is how we define insanity, then we must, therefore, re-define sanity as doing a different or new thing and expecting a new result. Habits of sanity then involve doing something new on a continual basis to move you to your desired end.

# Battling Change

It is said that we are the products of our *habits, thoughts and deeds*. A thought is an idea or opinion occurring in the mind, and deeds are intentional actions. A habit is defined as a recurrent, often unconscious pattern of behavior that is acquired through frequent repetition. It is also defined as an established disposition of the mind or character, according to the dictionary. There are several other definitions, but I will only focus on these two for the purpose of this book.

To summarize the meaning of a habit, we can say it is a recurrent pattern of behavior that is often unconscious and acquired through cultivated repetition. Putting everything together, we can then say we are the product of our thinking process and actions that come about through our recurrent behavioral patterns (habits) that are often unconscious and obtained through frequent repetition.

Throughout my research, one thing has been consistent in the recommendation of forming new habits. That thing is repetition. Conscious repetition eventually becomes unconscious repetition. From the day we are born, we learn through repetition. Our families, in fact, establish the routines that we may come to adopt throughout our lives. Remember my story of using my hands rather than the car defroster because that's what my father did all the time. Repetition, a technique used in schools, is the main reason for homework. Teachers want to give students more practice, especially if a lesson is part of a testing standard, so they assign homework to reinforce objectives.

Immediately, the questions become: "Can I change any or all of these (habits, thought or deeds) in order to change who I am? If I change just one aspect, will the other two still have significant impact? I know if I do nothing, then nothing will change. Therefore, I know my answer must be to begin with the catalyst, the one that impacts the others the most."

In chemistry, the catalyst is defined as a substance that causes or speeds up a chemical reaction without itself being changed. I am no chemist, but I took enough high school and college chemistry to realize that our thoughts best fit the description of the catalyst. Our thoughts, in fact, affect every aspect of our lives.

## Understanding Thoughts

Your desire to improve the quality of your life through re-scripting began as a thought. Thinking, or thoughts, are powerful and can't be overlooked in the process of re-scripting one's life and living your dreams. Thoughts are like text messages or emails. We use them for information transmission, but we don't know how they get from one source to the next.

Do you understand how email or text messaging works? I mean the actual science behind it. Does your lack of knowledge of how it works keep you from using it? Absolutely not! We use electricity even though

*Habits of sanity means doing something new on a continual basis to move you to your desired end.*

*~Suzette Clements*

it carries the risk of electrocution. We have been taught the proper use of these powerful forces of nature like electricity, but since there is still little physical evidence of thought, we often act as if power of thought is still only a theory.

When we use an iron to get the wrinkles out of our clothes, we never once stop to think of Ohm's law do we? We discussed Ohm's law in chapter 1. In review, it states that electrical current that passes through a conductor between two points is directly proportional to the potential difference across the two points. Scientific laws like these are not influenced by the subject upon which they act. They don't care if we are good or bad, happy or sad. They, like gravity, just are. They are neutral.

We discussed Feynman's double-slit experiment in chapter 2 that explains how an electron can act like either a particle or wave or both based on the opening through which it passes. Similarly, our thoughts about something varies based on the human sense (sight, touch, taste, hear, smell) that perceives it. Thus, perception is based on our interpretation of what we distinguish with our five senses.

When I conduct my seminars, I use the following illustration to make a strong point about perception. Six people are asked to stand around one person who is in the center. The five people are then instructed to stand around the center individual, who sits in a chair, in the following format. One person stands on each side, one in front, one behind, as well as one looking from the top and one looking from below. I then have one individual begin to describe the person in the center. I typically begin with the person who is standing in front. I then have the person who is in the back give a description, and so on until everyone has a chance.

Each person usually gives a lofty description of the same center individual, but they will all do it from there perspective, their viewpoint. The person looking at the front of the face will describe eyelashes and facial features. When the person standing in the back is asked if these things are correct, he or she will disagree and argue that the face is obscured, preventing an accurate description of the eyes, lips or nose. The two people on the sides will have similar descriptions as the person in front, but there may be some variation from left to right. Each observer of the center person gives a true description based on his or her point of view. If all are accurate in their description, is anyone more correct than another?

This little exercise shows how many possibilities there are when we use just one of the five senses, our eyes. If you add the other four senses, then the descriptions would vary even more. The descriptive possibilities would exponentially increase, just like the same electron passing through different openings. Just because we can't see something from our view or it doesn't stimulate our other four senses, doesn't mean it doesn't exist.

# The Power of Thought

For years, scientists studied light and looked for the medium through which light travels only to find that life creates its own medium. When we send a text or press the send button to send an email we have no clue how or through which medium it is sent. We only know how that it occurs. The invention of texting began in the 1980s, but the first actual texts was sent and received successfully December 12, 1992 using cellular signals in the UK. Neil Poppa sent the text message "Mary Christmas" to Richard Jarvis. Friedhelm Hillebrand and Bernard Ghillebaert invented the technology, protocol and rules that allow text messaging. At the age of 14, in 1978, V.A. Shiva Ayyadurai began building a system that we now know as "email," originally known as a Echo Mail. In 2004, Mark Zuckerberg, a college dropout, created Facebook.

I say all this to say that perhaps in the near future we will be able to measure or quantify the medium through which thought travels. Like the above inventors, no one ever thought that we would be able to do the things we now do, such as email, text messaging and Facebook. The possibilities are endless.

Inventors don't stop once they encounter an obstacle; they just keep reworking or retesting their concept until it works as they intended or close to it. Even once something is created and working, great inventors keep improving their concept. Likewise, you can keep reworking and retesting your thoughts until you establish an outlook that works for, rather than against, you. Once you establish effective thoughts, your habits and deeds will change accordingly.

Here is an example of changing a longstanding perception that will trigger a change in a person's eating habits:

*Before* – "I must eat everything on my plate."

*After* – "I can save some food for later or tomorrow."

It's incredible that I can send my sister Regna, who lives in Jamaica, a text and even video chat with her or play an Internet-based game while she is in her villa in Jamaica and I'm in Georgia. All the above is done in real time. We do not yet know the full potential of thought, but for now, we do know that it is an amazing and powerful medium to change one's behavior.

# Chapter 6 Written Exercise

Invent new ways to think about areas (i.e. health, hygiene, parenting, money management, communication) of your life that you need to improve the most. Invent means to come up with a totally different or even the opposite way of looking at a particularly undesirable situation or impression that you currently have. Here are some examples:

<u>Now</u>: All men are dogs.
<u>New</u>: I choose to see God (good) in all people.

<u>Now</u>: My children are lazy.
<u>New</u>: I have to establish clear expectations and accountability for my children.

<u>Now</u>: I never have time to work out or have fun.
<u>New</u>: I choose to schedule things that are a priority.

Now: _____

_____

New: _____

_____

Now: _____

_____

New: _____

_____

This next assignment will take 24 hours. For the next 24 hours, evaluate your habits. Determine where you are spending most of your time and energy. Keep in mind, your daily habits and choices get you from where you are today to your desired endpoint. Take this exercise seriously. Keep a log of the things that you do. Go to our website **HighestYou. com** to print out the "Daily Productivity Plan" worksheet on which you will log your habits for 24 hours. Write everything. Remember, the clearer your picture now, the clearer your future tomorrow. Write your DAILY TO-DO, WEEKLY TO-DO, REMINDERS (i.e. appointments and calls), and GOALS for today. Remember that your actions today determine your outcome tomorrow.

*"My actions today determine my outcome tomorrow."*

*~ Suzette Clements*

List seven bad habits you would like to get rid of. Once the habits are written, draw a line through the old bad habit and replace it with a new good habit.

1.  Old_____
    New_____

2.  Old_____
    New_____

3.  Old_____
    New_____

4.  Old_____
    New_____

5.  Old_____
    New_____

6.  Old_____
    New_____

7.  Old_____
    New_____

Take a deep breath here. Close your eyes and sit in silence for 10 minutes. Don't panic. This is simple. I will now teach you how to meditate. Once your eyes are closed the thoughts will flood in. Just allow them. Don't resist or try to control them. See them like cars passing by on a busy highway. They may come and go freely. They only have meaning because you have given them meaning. Soon your breathing will slow and some people sometimes perceive a light around their head. This has occurred several times for me but not every time. I often notice my eyes tend to become mildly tearful. Again, this is not every time, only sometimes. Once you have mastered 10 minutes twice per day, increase the interval to 20-30 minutes twice per day.

# 7

# THE POWER OF OUR DEEDS

As mentioned in the previous chapter, we are the products of our habits, thoughts and deeds. I will use the definition of deed as a noun rather than a verb. As such, deed is defined as an intentional act, one that is either good or bad. Let's review some of our intentional acts (deeds) that have become habits.

Have you ever noticed how the athletes of a particular sport have a similar physique? This is no coincidence. This is because they are using similar muscles in a repetitive manner. This repetition of action leads to the specific development of muscle groups and, therefore, body form. To excel in a sport, it's important to evaluate if you have the physique that is common to that sport. For instance, imagine a sumo wrestler playing tennis. As strong as he or she may be, that strength would not convert to the quickness and agility needed on a tennis court. Although there are exceptions to the rule, this generalization seems to be pretty obvious.

Olympic gold medalist Usain Bolt is too tall and lanky to have been considered a sprinter. However, despite not having the physique of a sprinter, he used the principle of the power of deeds to overcome his natural limitations. The take-home here is that no matter what, all things are possible. If you want to achieve something badly enough, you must, through repetition and habitual training, work for it. Despite insurmountable odds, Bolt's story is one of triumphant victory. He is an excellent example of how intentional acts, practicing your sport brings personal success. As we watch him crossing the finish line over and over, we witness the confidence with which he's become accustomed. To be considered the fastest man in the world, is a colossal achievement. This was not pure luck or genetic predisposition. It was one man who believed he could. This man saw the end from the beginning and scripted his life while preparing and persevering despite obstacles and shortcomings. He did not have the best in terms of training equipment and state-of-the-art facilities to practice. However, he did the best with what he had at the time, and his physical and mental commitment led him to become a champion.

# Happiness

What things are you telling yourself that are holding you back? I won't be happy until I get a new house. I won't be happy until I get straight A's. I won't be happy until I get a new car. I won't be happy until I lose weight. I won't be happy until I get that big promotion. I won't be happy until…. This list could go on and on. Stop right here. Take a

*Unbalanced systems soon show disease!*

*~ Suzette Clements*

deep breath now, and say the following: "I choose to be happy today. I choose to be happy this minute. I choose to be happy this second."

Happiness is not a destination; it is not found through people, things or situations. Happiness is an inward journey realizing that you have everything that you need. Happiness can only be experienced in the present. We can look fondly at the past or the future with gratitude and contentment, but happiness is a present moment experience. Try smiling in the past. This is possible; however, that's a subject for another book. If you think you won't be happy until X, Y and Z, then that will become your truth. Learn to be happy right now where you are. No matter what your life looks like right now, determine that everything is okay and all is well. Say, "It is well with my soul". I'm sure someone else would love to be in your shoes. As a podiatrist, I see tons of feet every year and a variety of foot and ankle conditions. Because I've seen a tremendous amount of foot and ankle complications over the past decade, I'm able to give perspective to patients on a daily basis. I often say to my patients that I use to complain about my feet until I met the man who had none.

## Balance

Our deeds or actions can also be a substitution for other problems. Often excess of any type is usually a cover up for other unresolved problems. Furthermore, excessive eating, excessive working, excessive playing, excessive buying, excessive talking, and even excessive praying can lead to problems. The point I'm making here is that any system out of balance will show disease. It doesn't matter what the system is, if it's too far to the left or too far to the right, it typically will become destructive or cause damage.

Seek balance and harmony. Seek to befriend people who have a habit in areas you want to incorporate in your life. Birds of a feather flock together. If you want to be healthy, befriend people who do healthy things. Become friends with them and pick up some of their good habits. Sign-up for a marathon. Join a support group. Join a sports team. Just do something! Take a step. Don't listen to all the reasons why you can't. Just move in the direction of where you want to go. Once you begin your journey, almost miraculously you will see new doors and opportunities open right in front of you. This is known as the corridor principle. It basically states that when you open a door in a corridor, as you walk down the hallway, other doors will open to you along your journey down the corridor.

# Chapter 7 Written Exercise

Sit quietly and take three deep breaths.

Smile and say, "I love my beautiful life"

List five intentional acts (deeds) you would like to begin doing such as exercising, joining a team, volunteering, singing, painting, playing an instrument, etc.

1. _____

2. _____

3. _____

4. _____

5. _____

# 8

# THE POWER OF PROPER PERSPECTIVE – NEW GLASSES

Perspective is like the mirrors or windows on a car. If the windows are dirty or if they are too tinted, everything we see is based on the view we have. The cleaner the window the better we can see where were going or even where we've been.

Have you ever been in a snowstorm where you could only clean off part of your window? Growing up in Cincinnati, snowstorms were a part of every winter. Coming from Jamaica, this was quite a huge transition for me. I remember using those ice scrapers to chisel the ice off the windows and only doing part of the window since I could not stand being in the frigid temperature for an extended time. My dad drove us to school every morning. He would often have to drive several miles before he had the entire windshield completely clean. He had an older model truck, which I believe appeared to be before defrosters were invented, so we had to do it the old-fashioned way. In order to get us to school on time, he would literally drive using one hand to clear the frost off the front window and the other hand to steer the truck. My mom never drove, so I couldn't pick up any good driving habits from her. Imagine if I never learned that the defroster was better than using my shirt sleeve, I may still be driving with one hand and wiping the windshield with the other. Looking back, I believe I started doing the same thing in college with my car until one day I saw the defrost button and decided to use it. I could hear the angels sing, but now they sang a little louder.

I left Cincinnati, Ohio, to go to college in Tulsa, Oklahoma. Talk about jumping out of the frying pan into the fire, except I jumped out of the fridge into the freezer. Driving in Tulsa without being able to see the road was horrendous. I believe God must've heard my prayer one day as I drove in frustration with the poor visibility through my windows. I couldn't see the road. I remember thinking, "I need a way to be able to see through the windows better." That day, I found the answer to my prayer. It was even built in. Yes, my very own front and rear view defroster. Those buttons had been there the entire time, but I never noticed them.

Often, we have the things that we need; we just don't realize that we have them. Dr. Candace Perth, a pharmacologist who in her early twenties, discovered the opiate receptor and significantly changed the world of neuroscience, sums it up best. She said, "We only see what we believe is possible." In

> *We only see what we believe is possible.*
>
> *~ Dr. Candace Perth*

my worldview, the defrost button was not in my scripting, so I was doing it the hard way. My way was very ineffective and could've been the cause of a devastating or fatal accident. My perspective was limited to only what I had perceived from my dad's actions.

## Perspective vs. Perception

Perspective is simply a point of view, our frame of reference. Perception deals more with how we recognize or interpret our sensory stimuli, which is anything that has an effect on or affects our five senses. A stimuli comes from the word stimulus, which is something which causes or evokes a reaction. Understanding this, we soon begin to realize that in order to properly re-script our lives, we must evaluate both our *perspective*, which is our viewpoint, and our *perception*, which is our interpretation of things.

The closer we are to a situation, the more limited our perspective. To see or evaluate a situation fully, it must be looked at from a wide or higher viewpoint. Rising above a situation requires the individual to see it from all angles. When flying, I'm often reminded how limited my perspective is while I'm on the ground. While on the runway, the plane seems to be going fast in preparing to take off, but in fact, the airplane is going slower than when we begin cruising at our desired altitude. Ironically, when the plane is in the air and cruising at a greater speed, things appear to be crawling on the ground when I stare out the window. This perspective was based on my sensory perception. This is an excellent example of the impact of perspective on our perception.

When we are able to step back from something and examine it from all sides, we gain a better perspective in order to gain a more accurate perception. On the runway of life, you may be running around in circles and asking yourself why you can't get anywhere. You may feel frustrated because your perception is limited and only shows you limited conditions around you. Dare to soar above the conditions in your life. See your life from a new perspective, a new viewpoint. This principle is also great when applied to how we view ourselves and others. Consider seeing from others perspective or viewpoint. Most arguments are founded on individuals arguing from only their perspective and interpretation, with little or incomplete facts.

My husband, Kirby Jr., is an amazing trial attorney. He uses the principles I'm stressing in this chapter on a daily basis. He uses the art of asking questions to get a better perspective. He examines all sides and angles, and this is where he soars like an eagle. The perception, which includes motives, intent and pre-meditation to name a few, is evaluated and dissected. Then comes the closing argument, which puts the entire situation into the proper context. The attorney who presents the best whole picture typically wins the favor of the jury and the judge. This due process allows for a frame of reference, as well as recognition and interpretation of the sensory stimuli, or the alleged act(s) in question. Fortunately, we don't have to go to three years of law school to learn these skills to effectively re-script our lives. Begin by using Kirby Jr's techniques. They work 100% of the time.

1. Ask leading, close-ended questions to lock down a particular point. These direct the witness in the direction he wants them to go. They can usually only be answered with "yes," "no" or other short, simplified responses. When done effectively, the person asking the question is effectively suggesting the answer.

   Here is an example of a close ended question. Suppose you suspected a child of eating all of the chocolate chip cookies, the questions might go like this:

   Q: Didn't I tell you not to eat the cookies?
   A: Yes.
   Q: You were just in the kitchen weren't you?
   A: Yes.
   Q: Those are cookie crumbs on your lips, aren't they?
   A: Yes.
   Q: You have cookie crumbs on your lips because you ate the chocolate chip cookies, didn't you?
   A: Yes

2. To get more information, begin with open-ended questions, also known as OEQ. These questions are designed to gather the most information. An open-ended question allows the other party to give an answer based on what they know?

   Suppose you are trying to figure out how a window was broken:

Q: Do you know who broke the window?

A: No.

Q: Were you present when it was broken.

A: Yes.

Q: What did you hear?

A: I heard someone yell out the number four?

Q: Who yelled out the number four?

A: Some guy outside with a stick

Q: When did he yell out "four"?

A: After he hit the ball with the stick.

Q: What kind of ball was it?

A: A golf ball.

Practice these questioning techniques often. Remember that asking questions leads to answers. Asking specific questions yields specific answers. We get what we ask for.

## Blaming vs. Reclaiming

Over the years, I have noticed that people who had ongoing turmoil in their lives were almost always focusing on or speaking about "other people" who were the source of their problems. It was either their husband, their wife, their child, their coworker or their boss. I remember a few were upset that their church would not pay their utility bill since they had been faithful members for years. They were all focusing on other people as the source of their problems. The stories were just that, stories. After several years of listening to the same stories over and over, I began suggesting that these patients begin to examine their own role in these relationships and work on improving themselves only. You would think I was giving away money. Patients started coming back with happier stories. Their physical pain that I had been treating began to improve in shorter periods of time. I began to decrease the strength of the corticosteroid injections I gave and replaced them with the words of empowerment and encouragement. The chronic foot conditions began to heal even faster.

I realize in my own life that when I accepted that I was both the problem and the solution and the situation was all in my control, my life took a drastic shift for the better. Things began to run more smoothly. I stopped trying to change other people and went about learning how to accept and improve me. I read just about every book on self-improvement that I could find. When reading a physical book was too slow, I would listen to motivational CDs and DVDs. I was learning so much information, but I wanted to learn faster. I was then introduced to audio books. I was ecstatic about having a book read to me while doing something else. Again, the angels sang, but now they were singing amazing. This was a beautiful experience. The more I learned, the more I realized I needed to learn. I also realized that I had a lot to unlearn.

For the life of me, I couldn't believe or understand why God would give me or anyone else such a task of changing other people. I noticed when I tried to get other people to believe the way I believed, I felt frustrated and often disappointed. I felt like a constant failure if they opted to keep their own belief systems. I finally realized that this was a losing battle. Again, I searched deep within my heart and began to read to find answers. None of it really made sense because I had a hard enough time managing me let alone other people and their stuff.

Along this journey to finding inner peace and strength, I found that I didn't have to carry this burden of improving other people or getting them to believe the way I believed. I just had to be the best me I knew to be. The lights came on. I began unloading the luggage of other people's stuff (OPS) I was carrying. I would always try to help others by removing what appeared to be there stumbling blocks, not realizing that they may have been stepping stones needed to take them higher.

I chose to learn to cast all my cares on God. They were not mine. In Christianity, we are taught that Jesus bore the weight of the world and died for our sins. Sins are properly defined as missing the mark. It didn't make sense that He would do all this work and yet I would still try to redo the work by carrying a burden that was not mine to carry or possible not even a burden at all. I once heard my mother-in-law ask, "Must Jesus bear the cross alone?" Then her answer was an astounding, "Yes." That's what He did. He bore the cross to restore us to a place as if we had not sinned or missed the mark. Evidently, a lot of us have not gotten this memo because we either beat ourselves up or beat others up based on our perception of them, which is heavily influenced by our perspective.

# Chapter 8 Written Exercise

1. Take three deep breaths and sit quietly.

2. On the lines below, write a problem that you're having difficulty solving.

   _____

   _____

   _____

   _____

   _____

3. Ask three acquaintances how they would solve the problem. If you're comfortable letting them know that it's your problem, that's perfectly fine. If not, tell them that you have a friend who has the following issue and you would like their advice on getting a result. You are not lying since you should be your own best friend. What you will notice is that they will come from a completely different perspective. Be open to their answers. Make sure you're asking both types of questions that we discussed earlier. Practice using both open-ended and leading questions.

4. Now separate yourself from this problem and ask yourself similar questions as if you're an outsider looking in. Look from the top of the problem, look from the left and right of the problem, and look from underneath the problem. Observe it from all sides.

Look to see if there is any possible good that could come out of the problem.

5. On the lnes below, write three possible good things that could come out of this problem.

_____

_____

_____

The art of learning to convert what appears to be bad into something good is one of the keys of living from a place of inner peace. This, I believe, is dwelling in the secret place. More on this in Chapter 11 when I discuss the power of playing.

# 9

# THE POWER OF COPYING

Don't reinvent the wheel. Learn from others and from nature. I am the first to admit that I have so much to learn. I believe life is a school that offers different courses and by a variety of teachers or instructors. Whether we see life as a game or as a continued educational experience is irrelevant. What is important is that we use the proper rules that apply to whatever route we choose. What do I mean by this? If you view life as a game, then it is vital to know the rules of the game of life. Can you imagine playing baseball with basketball rules? That would be quite comical, right? Well, this is often how we approach life.

It is said that most people plan more for vacation than they do for life. There is no school of life where you can major in healthy relationships or happy marriage 101. I would've loved the class called what to know before having a baby 101 or introduction to establishing work and life balance.

## Reading and Asking Questions

When we first got married, we seemed to argue about everything, and I mean everything. We were both establishing our boundaries while learning to compromise and respect each other's opinion. We were two strong-willed, opinionated individuals, working to live happily ever after. Quite honestly, I asked more questions about my major in college than I did about negotiating this phase of my life.

Even little tasks became huge deals. I remember when we decided to refinish our hardwood floor in the living room of our first home. This was a small, brick, ranch style house that we lived in after we got married. We decided to do the remodeling ourselves because it appeared fairly easy. Once we agreed on the color varnish we wanted to apply, we rented the machine to strip the varnish and buff the floors. The world was perfect until we finally started the project. Kirby Jr. is the left-brained, logical individual, and I am a right-brained, creative individual. My out-ofthe-box thinking with emphasis on imagination was now being challenged by logic and reasoning. These are concepts and words that I was vaguely familiar with. I was now being challenged to use all my brain. Can you imagine how difficult this was for me as my perfect newly-married world came to a squealing halt? I didn't need to analyze a task nor did I need a to-do-list. I was the master of winging it, and by gosh, it had gotten me everything I needed so far. Why would I now need to make such drastic changes? I functioned best by knowing the big picture, and Kirby kept focusing on every little detail. He even read the instruction manuals. "Oh my goodness," I thought, "we'll never get started at this rate, let alone finish before grandkids come over with their kids." The more he insisted on his detailed roadmap, I began realizing that he had quite a few valid points. From this experience was born our ability to begin appreciating each other's differences.

Throughout the years, we've come to realize that our combined opinions are better than each opinion standing alone. What we once saw as weaknesses in each other are now realized as strengths. This gives new meaning to the Scripture that speaks of the two becoming one. Since my right brain nature is to jump in with both feet in the deep end, asking questions later, I use his logical stepwise approach combined with my nature. I find this to be the best for both worlds. I can't speak for Kirby, but we've now been married for 22 years and together since age 19. Therefore, time and laughter in our home speaks volumes.

Early in our marriage, we read the book *"Men are from Mars and Women are from Venus,"* which shed tremendous light on our differences and allowed us to continue liking each other. How many of you know you can love someone but not like them? I soon began to use some of these methods and saw immediate improvement in all aspects of my life. When I had a problem, I began to ask questions. I either asked questions or read books from known experts on the topics. When we decided to start a family, I did just that. I purchased the book *"What to Expect When You're Expecting."* This book was such a lifesaver. When you're expecting your first child, there are so many choices and so many questions. I found there were so many well-meaning people giving faulty information. I would just say thank you for sharing with sincerity and cross-reference what they said with my book. It was a lifesaver.

## Getting a Mentor

Prior to completing my residency, I knew I wanted to start my own podiatry practice, but I had no clue where to start. I began asking questions. The more specific my questions, the more specific answers I received. I even met an amazing, well-seasoned doctor by the name of Hal Ornstein, who agreed to be my mentor. Hal is the founding president of the American Academy of Podiatric Practice Management and is in private practice in New Jersey. He is an amazing physician and individual with the most positive demeanor and charisma. He is all about helping other podiatrists become successful in their practice while giving exceptional podiatric care. He, along with Lynn Homisak, Owner, SOS Healthcare Management Solutions and Management Consulting and a certified podiatric medical assistant, came to my first office in 2002. They both assisted me in laying a firm foundation. Since I had no first-hand experience in private practice management, this was quite significant to me. Instead of trying to reinvent the wheel, I sought out an excellent mentor. For years, my staff teased me saying, "Hal, Hal, Hal…Whatever Hal says is all we hear." I followed their recommendations to the "T" and to the best of my ability. It's important to actually follow the advice of your mentor. Initially, our communications were frequent, as you can imagine how many questions I had. How do I bill for this? How do I hire? When and where do I purchase supplies, etc.? You name it, I asked it. Once I could hold my own, I needed less and less support until I found myself doing the same for new practitioners. You see, I realize how significant their mentorship was for me and my practice and when I asked Hal how I could ever repay him for his guidance, he smiled, gave me a big hug and said, "Just do the same for someone when you can." I have done just that.

If I ask if you want to be an excellent lawyer, what type of mentor would you look for? Your answer would be an excellent lawyer, right? Choose a mentor who produces constant fruit in the area where you want to bloom. If you choose a marriage counselor who has poor communication skills with his or her spouse or someone who never seems happy, you may find it difficult to get your desired end. Keep it simple. Do your homework and shop around. The basic foundational things such as integrity and honesty should not be overlooked in your research. Remember, the person you choose as your mentor will be given the right to influence an important aspect of your life, so choose wisely.

## Learning from Nature

Although people are excellent sources of knowledge, let's not forget the simple, everyday lessons we can learn from nature. Nature is all about seasons, balance, harmony, and interdependence. There are natural laws that are absolute. For example, each seed yields its own fruit.

Thus, a grain of corn never becomes an orange.

## We also have seasons.

An oak is a mighty tree, and its large roots grow deep and wide. It represents stability and a solid foundation. Even though it may have no leaves in the winter, be assured, come springtime, it will have new beautiful green leaves and produce more acorns. Like the oak, we have seasons. This is a natural process. It's important to realize that every season has its purpose. The cycle of life is necessary and will and must happen. As humans, we tend to become discouraged during the fall and winter seasons of our lives. Just because the leaves aren't green doesn't mean the tree is dead. Sometimes we have to just trust or have faith in the process, knowing all is well despite our perception.

Faith is the substance of things hoped for, and the evidence of things not seen (Heb. 11:1). Faith holds the big picture of your vision steady, allowing lesser things to fall way, "for in due season, you will reap if you faint not" (Gal. 6:9). In other words, keep the faith by focusing on your vision and doing what's necessary to bring about your desired outcome. Even though you aren't in the season where you can see the fruits of your labor, keep your focus on the vision while working toward it, and it will come to pass.

Several years ago, I noticed a beautiful plant growing in the front of our house. It was lodged between the concrete at the base of our step. I saw no dirt, however every year it would bloom the same beautiful pink petals. That flower reminded me to bloom where planted – even when I'm between two rocks, or as we say, "a rock and a hard place."

**"I choose to bloom where I'm planted."**

There is a solution for every problem, and an answer for every question. Your goal is to find the best source(s) for your answer. Then you must implement what you've learned by adopting through copying an expert's advice, principles or actions.

# Chapter 9 Written Exercise

1. Take three deep breaths and smile.

2. Practice inhaling for four counts and exhaling for four counts.

3. On each count, spell l-o-v-e. Inhale l-o-v-e over four counts, and exhale l-o-v-e over four counts. Do this in a rhythmic manner

4. Evaluate your life to see if you could benefit from a mentor. List at least three people who could serve as a mentor for you in specific areas of your life:

_____

_____

_____

_____

_____

_____

5. This is a quick and easy exercise to stay focused or to refocus on the vision. Remember, our five senses don't determine the outcome. What we sense only helps our interpretation. Remember chapter 8 on perspective? Apply what you learned here. Widen your perspective and see all the seasons of your life.

6. Plan a one-hour walking meditation outside. This is to be done in complete silence. Walk slowly and quietly observe the trees, the grass, any insects or even the wind

as it blows. If possible, stand still and watch an insect for about 10 minutes. What are some lessons you can learn from this experience. These things in nature are also your mentors. Can you see yourself as the mighty oak? Notice how even though strong winds blows, it still stands firm. Notice how graceful the butterfly goes about collecting pollen and spreading beauty? What aspects of life could you see in the butterfly? Do you make it a habit to go about spreading joy and happiness into the lives of other people? Notice the grass and how it gently sways from side to side. It's flexible. Can you see this quality in yourself? There so many things we can learn from nature, so observe and write down your thoughts.

# 10

# THE POWER OF KNOWING YOU

Who are you? Most people mistakenly define themselves by their occupation (i.e. teacher, lawyer, chef) or given role in life (i.e. husband, wife, daughter, father). Being a nurse, for instance, is not who you are; that's what you do. While what you do for a living may give you some indication as to who you are, it still does not adequately address your identity. Likewise, taking on a role – whether voluntarily adopted or inherently given – fails to properly address the question of who you are.

Why is this step so important? Imagine a young boy being lost at carnival. When the child is asked his name, he can easily respond. Simply knowing his name can help others to get him back to his parents. Now suppose the child didn't know his name. All he knew was what he liked to do, such as "play soccer," and his role, for instance, as a "little brother." To take this a step further, suppose he didn't know his parents' names, or to whom he belonged.

The latter scenario of the lost child is how many of us go through life. We don't know our names (who we are), but we can quickly tell you what we do or our role. Meanwhile, others don't even know their source, or parentage. As such, many seemingly successfully professionals remain frustrated and miserable because of their displaced or unknown identity. They have spent their entire lives doing what their family, community or society expected them to do without any consideration as to who they truly are. This disconnect typically leads to pervasive discontent and self-destructive tendencies, such as excessive drinking, prescription drug addiction and so forth. We have all probably heard of people leaving high-powered, high-paying positions because they wanted to do mission work, become a mechanic, or simply spend more time raising their kids. Remember, this book is about finding happiness, not necessarily wealth and fame, which may come as a result but is not the main goal. We are seeking soul satisfaction by acknowledging our source and our identity.

## Being Rather Than Doing

Effectively re-scripting your life requires that you know who you are. In chapter 5, we discussed how other people's negative input can cause us to think falsely about ourselves, sometimes causing us to adopt the wrong name

(i.e. lazy, stupid, ugly). Once you erase and abandon that scripting, you must seek clarity about "being" rather than "doing" in order to successfully re-script. This may be a challenge because our society focuses almost entirely on doing. Even as a child, when adults ask, "What do you want to be when you grow up?" they actually mean, "What do you want to do when you grow up?"

When Moses asked God for His name so he could tell the Israelis who was giving him this authority, God answered, tell them "'I AM" has sent you (Exodus 3:14). God's reply was about being, not a specific moniker that coincided with what He does or can do. Keep in mind, the word "am" is a form of the verb "to be." God knows how to assign meaningful names, as he did by changing Jacob's name to Israel, but His own name describes who He is collectively, not what He does routinely.

## Habit of Doing

Most people do things because that's the way it's always been done. Why make life challenging by trying to do something differently? Suppose, however, you could improve your life and relationships by doing things differently. Even then, some people would rather stay where they are than seek or make an attempt to change. If you're reading this book, this is not your mindset, though.

We are creatures of habit, a routine of behavior that is repeated regularly and tends to occur unconsciously. For instance, we create a habit of brushing our hair, brushing our teeth, and washing our hands. These habits were introduced in early childhood and reinforced by well-meaning parents and caregivers until they became routine and automatic.

I remember how concerned we were when our young son continually failed to use his fork and knife properly at the dinner table. It got really bad. For the longest, my husband's "go to" statement to him at the dinner table was "eat like a human being son." Looking back now, it's almost comical to see how much energy we spent on this one habit. Plenty of the dinnertime hours were focused on this one topic. Ironically, once we allowed him to do the modified version of what worked best for him, the struggle disappeared. We allowed him to be.

Appreciating his uniqueness in using his utensils allowed mealtime at the Clements to be fun and full of precious bonding moments versus constant criticism and critique. Further revelation came when one of his friends came to our house for dinner. They were both in the third grade and eating as quickly as possible so they could get back to their Runescape internet games. To our amazement, Tiger and Michael held their cup and utensils almost identically to little Kirby. One by one, friend after friend, we noticed a similar awkwardness in regard to holding utensils. He had been eating like a human being after all. At age 8, he was doing the best with the muscle power and hand coordination that he had for his developmental age.

Good habits are best formed when age-appropriate limitations are considered. When I instruct older patients to begin moving (exercising), I take into consideration their possible physical limitations. I actually recommend that they play versus exercise. I'll explain this concept in the next chapter. Because the idea of *being* healthy had eluded them, I recommend they get into the habit of *doing* something, anything that they can manage safely and enjoy. Thinking outside the box really helps here. Chair exercises are great, for instance. Sitting in a chair and holding a can of vegetables in each hand and doing arm raises can engage the core muscles and increase mental clarity and alertness. I often tell them, "If you don't use it, you lose it." This concept applies to anything. I call this the principle of disuse.

Establishing habits of healthy moving is often overlooked by most well-meaning adults as they mature. Society

*The Principle of Dis-Use:*
*"If you don't use it, you lose it."*

*~ Suzette Clements*

tells us that as we age, we become weaker and more fragile. Although some of this may be true, it is not true for everyone. There are many cultures where older, mature individuals live to be physically active well into their 80s and 90s.

Habits are significant. The habit of doing, at least physically or mentally, is significant since a substantial amount of diseases are caused by limited or lack of physical activity or proper mental health. Systems of healthy habits produce living in divine health. Systems of wealthy habits produce financial freedom. If you want to be healthy, you must practice healthy habits. If you want to be wealthy, you must practice habits of wealth. Furthermore, habits of happiness, produce happiness. Like choices, habits are the bricks that lay the foundation of the house. Ask yourself: "What are the habits that I am using to produce my house?" Keep in mind, though, doing should never overshadow the need to be, which should direct most of what we do.

# Learning to Be

We know what to do because we are always being told either from the law, supervisors, doctors, or parents, but no one except God can or should tell you who you are. Who we are comes to us naturally. It makes us comfortable and happy. If this identification seems so simple, why do so many people have trouble answering this question effortlessly? Again, society's emphasis is on doing. We even get rewarded for *doing*, usually not *being*. From the time we begin school, we get rewarded for getting good grades, having perfect attendance, and winning games. We even get punished for not doing. No one gets rewarded in elementary school for *being* a giver, advocate, humorist or even a fighter.

Sometimes saying who you are not is an effective means of beginning this process of identity declaration. In fact, most people can spout off who they are not more easily than who they are. The goal here is to move toward the mindset of true self-discovery. When asked, "Suzette, who are you?" I would say the following:

Previously, I would instinctively say "a podiatrist" or maybe "a mother" and "a wife" too. However, that does NOT answer the question. Being a podiatrist is what I do, not who I am. I am *a facilitator* of health in the natural and spiritual. I do this in being a wife, mother and doctor, formerly a nurse, and now I am doing it as an author, artist and speaker/coach.

Once you accurately identify who you are, you will likely find that you have already had some interest or connection with who you truly are. For instance, if you say that you are an "advisor," you may realize that you have spent considerable time listening and providing solid advice to friends and family. People may even routinely come to you for direction and suggest that others do too. Meanwhile, you may be working as a banker or baker, in careers that having nothing to do with who you are. Still, the advisor in you likely emerges on the job, as you counsel those around you. Similarly, who you truly are may involve a hobby that you do on the side. The point is that you discover you and allow you to manifest in some form. This will lead to your life's satisfaction and happiness.

# Chapter 10 Written Exercise

Sit quietly and take a deep breath. Smile and say, "It is well." You may want to pray for or meditate on spiritual direction in completing this exercise.

1. Who are you? Do NOT include your occupation, responsibilities or family roles. If this is too difficult right now, skip to the next exercises in this chapter about your favorite things to do and how they may relate, AND THEN come back to this exercise.

   _____

   _____

   _____

   _____

   _____

   _____

   _____

   _____

2. List your five favorite things to do or that you do well:

   1._____

   2._____

   3._____

   4._____

   5._____

3. List ways that what you like to do relates to who you are:

1._____

2._____

3._____

4._____

5._____

# 11

# THE POWER OF PLAY

As kids, we have a natural tendency to play, laugh, run, jump, build, and demolish. When upset, we pout and cry at the drop of a hat. Children are true authentic beings. They are authentic, at least, until we adults get our grubby hands on them. We, as a society, begin the molding process to help kids "fit" into society.

As kids mature, playing is soon replaced with exercising. They are not the same, though. Exercise is a means to an end. Play, however, creates pleasure, laughter and fun along the way. Playing keeps you in the present moment while exercise is often motivated by the past or future. In the past, you may have been told that you will need high blood pressure medications or insulin for diabetes control if you don't lose weight. So now you force yourself to jump on a treadmill like a mindless hamster so you won't develop these diseases. As bad as that is, you may now want to get back down to your college size, but your mind begins telling you this is impossible or may require too much of you. Immediately, you begin using statements such as, "What if I can never lose the weight? What if I start developing other diseases? What if I already have other diseases and don't know yet?" The flood of what ifs become overwhelming. You then become stuck in the what if cycle, forgetting that you can achieve your health goals while enjoying life without worry. You can do this through play.

# Learning to Play Again

Watching my little nephew Jeffery play with his train set is such a pleasure. He is perfectly engaged while driving the trains back and forth. He jumps, laughs, and makes sounds, as he is in his perfect little world. Even eating appears to be a distraction for him while playing. Asking him to sit and eat an entire meal while being unable to play almost seems cruel. He typically hurries through his meal, leaving half on the plate to get back to his world of imagination and play. Never once does his mom or dad have to tell him to focus when he's playing. He does it automatically.

One of my older nephews, Daniel, just produced his first album. He is a self-taught guitar player and a singer songwriter. At any given time, Daniel can be seen toting his guitar around or strumming like Willie Nelson. He is a beautiful songwriter and does so with such passion and purpose. While in college, he seemed to blossom in this regard. No one had to call him and remind him to practice. It became automatic. It became a pleasure. It became a part of him. He uses the power of playing as a young adult to share his message of being true to yourself and authentic. How powerful is that? Recently, I listened to a song he wrote and recorded that is now being played on a Canadian and American radio stations. To listen to his songs go to http://www.reverbnation.com/jandones

As a child, I loved to paint and draw. In December 2013, I went to a shoe store and saw a beautiful hand-painted picture on the wall. I asked the cashier who painted it, and she said that she had. Somewhat awkwardly, I asked if it was for purchase because it reminded me so much of my childhood. She states that she is a new painter and was just doing it for fun. She sold me the picture for $25 and wrapped it up for me. As I walked out of the store, I felt like a kid in a candy store. That one little picture became a catalyst in my life. Immediately outside the door of the store, the store next to the shoe store was called "Sue Ye Fine Art." I thought that was a sign from God. You can even use a Jamaican accent and sound like my dad. I was so tickled. I placed the picture on my wall and it brought me much happiness.

The actual store sign is pictured above

Recently, I began taking an art class, and I had a Russian instructor named Paulina who helped me reconnect with the child artist within me. The artwork I produced since learning to play again is displayed on our website at HighestYou.com under, "The Art of Happiness". What I found is that when I am painting, it's as if all time stands still. I find it to be peaceful, and it brings immense pleasure. I also find my art itself to be cheerful and childlike, which is exactly how I feel when I'm creating it.

Like my nephew Jeffery, I find myself wanting to get back to my painting as quickly as possible. No one has to tell me to go do it. It's something I enjoy doing so much that I wake up early to look at what I've created the night before. I feel like a child the night before Christmas. I even find that I have to put myself on a painting timeout so I can get my other chores done.

## Finding an Enjoyable Outlet

The take home here is to replace exercise (helpful tasks) with play (beneficial fun). Become like a little child. Playing releases endorphins, which are nature's morphine. Play encourages communication, corporation and comradery. There is something powerful about being a part of a sports team or amongst others with the same interest who also enjoy doing what you do.

We have a cousin named Theodora who recently lost her husband my uncle Stanley by marriage. She grieved for a season after his death, but she soon found her stride again. She is enjoying her newfound play of ballroom dancing. Often people become sad and depressed after losing a loved one. She, however, made a choice to jump right back into life. She is vibrant, energetic and a pleasure to be around because of it.

Consider joining a sports team or joining a group that caters to a specific hobby. Try one you liked in school or try something new. For instance, take a ballroom dance class, learn golfing or even go hiking. Play pool or go swimming in a pool. Sign up for a class of water aerobics or yoga. Try an African dance class. There are plenty of local activities in every community. If you search, you will find something.

# Chapter 11 Written Exercise

Plan to play every day. Here are some ideas:

1. Learn or relearn how to play an instrument. Go to YouTube and search for instructions on playing an instrument. Both my kids taught themselves how to play the piano and guitar by watching online videos. They had some formal training, but the majority of their achievement was from what they learned on YouTube.

2. Take a class, such as art, of some kind or join a group that involves an activity of your interest.

3. Teach a class on something that you know well and enjoy doing. Once I began painting, I was asked to teach acrylic paint classes within five weeks of my first session. I now teach The Art of Happiness at Emory University Continuing Education and I am having the time of my life.

4. Ask your kids what they want to do. Kids are full of fun ideas of how to play. They are always asking us to join them, but we are often too busy with life. The best vacations we've had as a family has been either my daughter or son's recommendation. Be prepared, though. This could mean doing handstands in a pool.

# 12

# THE POWER OF OUR WORDS

In chapter 1, we discussed that we are made in the image of God, the great I AM. Well, just how God spoke and it became, we too have the power to do the same. Our words become things; they take on life. If you don't believe me, go to your nearest gas station and ask for a bottle of water. I guarantee someone will point you to the water. Once you pay for it, you will then have it in your possession.

If my children ask me for a drink, I would give it to them as long as I knew it would not harm them. God envisions the same for us. When we pray, we are asking God to do something. Like a loving parent, He wants to give us the desires of our heart while being MINDFUL that some desires may cause harm if given prematurely or in the wrong season.

It doesn't end there. Notice that some action was required on my part. After asking for the water, I had to move in the direction of where I was instructed it would be. This is a key point. We often pray then stop there. My father-in-law, Dr. Kirby Clements Sr., who is also a bishop, often says, "God won't do for you what He intends for you to do for yourself."

We often wait for God to do for us not realizing He is wanting to work through us. If we believe that God gives us the desires of our hearts, then we must also believe that we are able to have our hearts desires and thus act in faith.

Knowing this, the questions become: What is my part in this co-creation? What do I need to do? Who can I align with? How are my thoughts? How are my beliefs? Do I say one thing and believe another? Do I have supportive habits that bring me closer to my dreams? Do I speak life or death over my daily affairs? If life and death are truly in the power of the tongue, how am I using my tongue? Is it producing life or is it producing death? Finally, ask yourself the following question: If my words became alive as I spoke them, how carefully would I choose them? Whether you accept this or not, things happen based on what we say – to ourselves and others.

## Speaking to the End

Remember in chapter one, I recommended that before beginning any journey, it's imperative to begin where you want to end. You should ask questions such as: What will my life look like this time next year and five years from now? What will my life look like if I continue doing what I am currently doing? If I want better for myself or my loved ones, where do I begin?

I and other physicians use a method that has worked for decades. When a patient presents to my office they go through a process. The process involves asking questions as to what is happening that brings them to my office. After that initial interview by my medical assistant, I introduce myself and asked more questions. As a physician, I use this process called "SOAP." This stands for subjective, objective, assessment and plan. The patient comes into my office with a problem and I listen to his or her story. The story is also known as "the subjective." I then do my evaluation, which is "the objective." This is followed by formulation of my assessment, or the diagnosis. The plan is the final part of this process. The plan represents the action that I or the patient will need to take to get the desired outcome.

When I create a treatment plan for a patient, I use the same principles discussed in this book. I and the patient determine an end destination. The typical end destinations are: walking pain free; returning to a state without skin disease, such as fungus or infection in the lower extremity; and eliminating calloused lesions or ulcerations in the foot or ankle. The treatment plan for successfully re-scripting our lives must include affirming words that focus on the end we seek , not our current situation.

## The Body's Reaction to Words

Dr. Masaru Emoto is a Japanese author who purportedly exposed distilled water to different words, pictures, music, and prayers to determine if they could affect the water's crystal formation when frozen. Emoto suggested that water exposed to positive energy (speech, etc.) would result in "beautiful" crystals when frozen, and negative energy would produce "ugly" frozen formations. Water treated with the song *Amazing Grace* and the words "thank you" produced full crystals while water treated with words like "you fool" and "you disgust me" showed no crystal formation. Although this famous experiment does not make sense to my natural mind, the possibilities are hopeful and endless. When the Wright brothers had multiple failed flights after flights, they kept focused on the vision and the end destination. Now flying is a common occurrence. Trail blazers like Dr. Emoto and The Wright Brothers are often the recipients' of criticism and ridicule. We are conditioned to only see what we believe is possible so when new thoughts and ideas come our way our old programming can keep us from seeing the greater good in these new ideas and inventions.

Most literature agrees that our bodies are composed of greater than 70% water. The power of words to produce tangible changes in our bodies is more significant than we currently know, understand or believe. Words begin reactions within our bodies. Our bodies have similar reactions to water when spoken to or receiving positive or negative input.

Try this quick experiment. Close your eyes and imagine that someone just gave you a glass of pure lemon juice. There's no sugar in it and no water. Imagine that you now have the lemon juice in your mouth. What are you experiencing? Are the sides of your jaws puckering? Is your mouth watering because you're beginning to salivate? Are you squinting your eyes because of the tartness of the sour taste of the lemon? That simple experiment shows how the power of thought can cause a chemical reaction within your body. There are enzymes in our mouth that are released when certain foods are introduced. Although the foods or not actually introduced in this experiment, the mere thought produces the same reaction. The same reaction would occur if someone described this scenario and you began to think about it because in your mind, you envisioned taking the lemon juice into your mouth. How powerful was that?

The Apostles Creed says, "Let the words of my mouth and the meditation of my heart be acceptable in thy sight, Oh LORD, my strength and my redeemer" (Psalm 19:14). The meditation of my heart is comparable to the program that is running on the hard drive of the computer. What we dwell on is what we meditate on. If our words and meditations are to have a positive impact on our bodies and our lives, they must be positive in nature. I believe this is why the Scripture tells us to, "Speak the things that aren't as though they were" (Rom. 14:7). This is not lying or self-deception. You are basically speaking to the water molecules in your body and allowing them to form new, beautiful crystals. Life is not about trying to be perfect, it is awakening to the perfection you already are, the perfect masterpiece that you're made to be.

## Speaking to God

"Re-Scription" is basically treating yourself as if you are the water molecule that becomes the beautiful crystal. In the process of re-scripting, I recommend meditation and prayer as routine activities. In order to accomplish this effectively, we must take time to unplug. This means sitting quietly and learning to be at peace with yourself. Remember that prayer and meditation are a two-way flow that allows for the constant flow to and from the Divine. Both are crucial for our spiritual beings to stay connected with our Divine source. We are conduits through which this beautiful power, spirit and anointing flows. This keeps us connected to the greater power that is within us. Meditation is NOT a religion. It is simply sitting quietly and unplugging from the noise of our own chatter and the chatter of others. It allows us to reboot our mind and recharge our batteries. When we unplug from external stimuli, we automatically plug into our source, our divine intelligence, who I define as God.

For years, I kept the following statement on my office wall, and it still hangs there:

*"In quietness and confidence shall be your strength."*

Whenever things in my life appear to be chaotic and out of balance, I always glance at that sign because those words automatically help me redirect and re-center. As a Christian, I know the power of prayer in my own life. As a physician, I witness the power of prayer in the lives of my patients. There have been multiple studies that have been done to show that prayer and meditation have tangible effects on individuals and situations.

Dr. Herbert Benson is a Harvard scientist who has studied prayer and meditation and their effect on the body for 30 years. He says all forms of prayer induce a relaxation response that reduces stress, calms the body, and promotes healing. Dr. Benson has even documented the physical changes seen on MRI brain scans that occur in the body when someone meditates. The body becomes relaxed and physiological activity also becomes more evenly regulated, according to an article titled "Can Prayer Heal?" The same article discusses Dr. Harold Koenig, associate professor of medicine and psychiatry at Duke, who says traditional religious beliefs have a variety of positive effects on health. In his *Handbook of Religion and Health*, he documented nearly 1,200 studies on prayer and the effects on health. The studies showed:

- Hospitalized people who never attended church have an average stay of three times longer than people who attended regularly.
- Heart patients were 14 times more likely to die following surgery if they did not participate in a religion.
- Elderly people who never or rarely attended church had a stroke rate double that of people who attended regularly.

If you recall in chapter 3, I referenced prayer as equivalent to the venous (vein) system returning deoxygenated blood to the heart, representing God, and meditation being the arterial (artery) system, which brings oxygenated blood away from the heart. Oxygen is the vehicle through which life and nutrients are supplied to the organs via the blood. I view the blood as the vehicle or median through which this communication takes place. The blood, in my perspective, is that spiritual nature or being that allows constant communication with our infinite spirit.

You must develop your own form of prayer based on your belief system. Develop your own form of meditation, or stillness, based on your belief system. Go back to chapter 1 and rewrite your vision. Now make it bigger. Dream bigger! Dare to dream so big that when it comes to life you know that it was through the power of God working in and through, you the conduit.

## Finding Your Path

We are all a part of the whole. No one part is greater than the other. We, as human beings, are all made in the image of God. No one is greater or lesser. We are all equal. The Scripture says how can we love God who we have not seen and yet hate our neighbor who we see (1 John 4:20). As long as we continue to see others as greater than or less than us, we will continue to miss the mark, or sin. God is not a religion. God simply is.

We are all God's children, the body of Christ consciousness. We are simply different expressions of the same divinity. Like the physical body, there are different organ systems that belong to the same head. At no time does the left hand say to the right foot you are not significant. They may have different roles, yet they are still significant for the body. The body parts are all a part of the body, but maintains their identity. My current belief is that I can also choose to maintain my identity and still be a part of the whole. "Being One" does not mean one religion or one belief system. "Being One" means being the best part of the whole that you can be. If you are a hand, be the best hand you can be and help the whole body by being what you were created to be. Bloom where you are planted. It is my belief that Dis-Ease is accelerated when we forget our purpose or identity. Imagine the hand acting like the knee? We do this when we compare ourselves to others or lose our path, vision, passion or purpose.

Our physical nature is here today and gone tomorrow. However, I believe that our spirit is never born and never dies, which makes us amazing eternal spiritual beings. Periodically, we peep through the veil and see the miraculous, but because it frightens us, we shun away from it. What if we could walk in our Christ consciousness while dwelling in our physical bodies? Could we then begin to do greater things than Jesus did and as he mandated us to do? Could we be able to feed 5,000 without working a 9-5? Could we turn water into wine? I believe that we can and are equipped to do these things. If it were not possible we would not have been told to do it. If we connect or become synchronized with our divine intelligence, then the miracles and manifestations would become second-nature or everyday happenings.

I believe Jesus Christ shared principles for life, and thus, I endeavour to do the same. I do not see religion as right or wrong. I see human beings attempting to make sense of their external world. If God is the head or the supreme consciousness, than we are the body. We, human beings, are all a part of this body. Therefore, I embrace who I am, and I believe that my journey will help someone else along their journey. I believe if I was born in another country and raised in another religion, I may be writing this book from a totally different religious perspective but having the same conclusion. So again, my intention in writing this book is not to convert you to Christianity or any other religion, but to help you realize that you have the power to find your own path. That power lies within you. It always has and it always will. Happiness cannot be found in possessions or money. Happiness is an inward journey realizing that you are complete and whole just the way you are. It lies in living from a place of integrity and honesty while being self actualized.

Living an amazing life means different things to different people because people define success differently. Take this time to define what is most important to you. I asked my teenage daughter if she had the option between success and happiness which one would she choose. She said to be successfully happy. I must say I agree with her 100%. Often we chase after material things or status believing they will bring us happiness only to acquire these things and still feel empty.

The point is to be true to your own heart. Use your intuition, your spiritual being, or the Holy Spirit, as a guide as you are moving throughout your day and life. This inner guidance is like a GPS system. It is very specific but only works when it has a signal. When the signal is lost, you become lost. You may drive around for hours, arrive late to your destination or miss your destination altogether. If you have continuous channels of communication, then you will have no lost signals and move along your desired path. Obstacles may come. Some may be red lights telling us to stop momentarily or yellow lights cautioning us to slow down.

If you notice, when you're on a long journey, you may not hear anything for a while from your GPS system. You may even need to check the GPS to make sure it still navigating you in the proper direction. As spiritual beings, we are no different. We function best when we are in constant communication with our infinite being. If you are of person of religious orientation, believe with all your heart. Whatever you decide is your belief, ensure that it produces life and love, not death and hatred. Search your heart. Ask questions. Read books. Strive to be the best you can be. Speak life. I still have many unanswered questions in my heart and mind, for there are

*Father, Forgive me for forgetting who you created me to be. Thank you for reminding me who I AM.*

*Love,*
*Suzette*

many theories and doctrines. Always search your heart. Find your truth. Choose to be happy meanwhile. Don't wait on circumstances or people to make you happy. Happiness is realized the moment you synchronize your habits, thoughts and deeds with your belief systems and intentions, thus manifesting your true, fully-actualized self.

# Chapter 12 Written Exercise

In the process of Re-Scription, constructive words become key. These are the following words that I strongly recommend that you print and memorize, allowing them to run on your hard drive. Remember, life is about giving and receiving, and we are conduits or vessels of this beautiful thing called life. As long as we have life in our bodies, we still have a purpose.

For more information on the Re-Scription process, go to HighestYou.com for the Meditation Made Easy CD, as well as Coaching, and ordering your own Re-Scription Movie. Remember: Re-Scription takes the thought, converts it to a written vision then converts it to a movie of the new vision which becomes actualized as living the dream as you become the dream.

Re-Scription process:

| Thoughts, Dreams, Ideas | 1D (one dimensional) |
|---|---|
| Written Vision | 2D (two dimensional) |
| Movie of Vision | 3D (three dimensional) |
| Living the Vision | 4D (four dimensional) |
| Become the Vision | 5D (five dimensional) |

As you re-script your life, allow the following statements to assist you in re-creating a life that is purposeful, successful, productive, and HAPPY. Re-script your life such that it brings you self-actualization and enjoyment while allowing you to dwell in a secret place of peace, happiness and abundance.

Memorize the affirmations below and say them daily as you would take a vitamin. Create your own. Have fun. Dream Big! Share with others. Go for it. I BELIEVE IN YOU. You can do this!

I am a human being happy

I am a human being favored.

I'm a human being healthy.

I am a human being self-actualized.

I'm a human being giving grace.

I'm a human being authentic.

I'm a human being receiving love.

I'm a human being giving love.

I'm a human being appreciative.

I'm a human being receiving grace.

I'm a human being appreciating.

I'm a human being receiving favor.

I'm a human being grateful.

I'm a human being accepting others.

I'm a human being unselfish.

I'm a human being a blessing.

I'm a human being free from criticism.

I'm a human being free from condemnation.

I'm a human being casting my fears.

I'm a human being living in a state of abundance

I'm a human being accepted.

I'm a human being loving.

I'm a human being living in the state of integrity.

I'm a human being divine.

I'm a human being joyful.

I'm a human being casting my cares.

I'm a human being peaceful.

I'm a human being lovely.

I'm a human being thoughtful.

I am that I am.

# Note from the Author

I sincerely pray that the words from this book have opened your eyes to begin or further see clearly through the veil of illusion that we have created. May you see that you are a magnificent spiritual being who has the ability through choice and habits to dream big and live life to the fullest. May you learn early to convert every defeat and difficulty into stepping stones and building blocks of the magnificent you. May you find true happiness and self-actualization, being both authentic and passionate living from a place of hope, peace, integrity, and love.

A Human Being choosing to be happy,
*Suzette*

# References

Can Prayer Heal?
> http://www.webmd.com/balance/features/can-prayer-heal Retrieved May 2014

Covey, Stephen R.. *The 7 Habits of Highly Effective People*. S.l.: Must Read Summaries, 2011.

Goddard, Neville. *Feeling is the Secret*. New York: Goddard Publications, 1944.

Hill, Napoleon. *Think and Grow Rich* original 1937 edition. S.l.: Duke Classics, 2012.

Ruiz, Miguel. *The Four Agreements: A Practical Guide to Personal Freedom*. San Rafael, Calif: Amber-Allen Pub. :, 1997.

Shinn, Florence Scovel. *The Game of Life and How to Play It*. Marina del Rey, Calif: DeVorss, 1925.

Made in the USA
Columbia, SC
26 December 2024

50624350R00087